TOWERS, SPIRES AND PINNACLES

Towers, spires and pinnacles

*A history of the cathedrals and churches
of the Church of Ireland*

Sam Hutchison

Wordwell

First published in 2003
Wordwell Ltd
PO Box 69, Bray, Co. Wicklow
Copyright © The author

Cover design: Rachel Dunne

ISBN 1 869857 57 7

British Library Cataloguing-in-Publication Data.
A catalogue record for this book is available from the British Library.

This publication has received support from the Heritage Council under the 2003
Publications Grant Scheme.

Typeset in Ireland by Wordwell Ltd.

Editor: Emer Condit.

Book design: Nick Maxwell.

All photographs by the author unless otherwise stated.

Printed by E.G. Zure, Bilbao.

Contents

Foreword

Some years ago I drew attention in the General Synod to the fact that most of our churches were without a photographic record.

This lack has now been marvellously filled by Mr Hutchison, who in his retirement has visited and photographed all our churches in the Republic and a good number in Northern Ireland as well.

He has now written a book which gives the fruit of this research and I am most happy to commend it. Many of our churches are of the highest quality and yet are largely unvisited owing to their remote settings. I hope that many will use this book to seek them out.

How they are to be maintained in the future is another question. In a recent letter in the *Church of Ireland Gazette* I drew attention to the extremely haphazard distribution of State aid. Given the fact that St Mary's Youghal has received nothing and that the very small cathedral of Kilfenora is to receive one million euros it is hard not to suspect an entirely political motivation.

Robert MacCarthy
Dean of St Patrick's Cathedral

Preface

There are a number of worthy books dealing specifically with church architecture in Ireland, of which *The cathedrals of Ireland* by Peter Galloway and *The churches and abbeys of Ireland* by Brian de Breffny and George Mott are among the best. There are also those which deal with a particular church, such as *A history of Christ Church Cathedral*, edited by Kenneth Milne. However, there is no single volume telling the story of the churches and cathedrals of the Church of Ireland and the aim of this book is to fill that gap.

In 2000 there were approximately 1100 churches still open for worship (650 in the Republic and 450 in Northern Ireland). These range from the medieval cathedrals and ancient parish churches in the care of the Church of Ireland since the Reformation to the medley of new churches built in eastern Ulster during the second half of the twentieth century. Except for the medieval period it is not possible to include them all, and many beautiful, well-loved and well-cared-for churches have had to be omitted. Only a brief description of those chosen is possible, and as a result the large cathedrals receive more or less the same space as an interesting but little-known country church. The former are, in any event, already well documented.

I commenced this task following retirement in 1992 and for the next nine summers travelled over 18,000 miles and photographed more than 850 churches. Many, especially in the south, are memorials to a civilisation and way of life that no longer exist. The Anglo-Irish aristocracy in the eighteenth, nineteenth and early twentieth centuries had their faults but lack of taste was rarely one of them, and this is reflected in the many lovely churches handed down to us. Not all are beautiful but even the plainest frequently has a certain charm, not least because of its location. When known, the date of consecration (or completion) and the name of the architect of each church are indicated after its name. Until about the middle of the eighteenth century the architect is rarely known and this is also true of those churches built in the early nineteenth century, which form the nucleus of those still in use.

Visiting these churches has been a wonderful experience, involving journeys to remote and little-known parts of the country seldom seen by tourists. People everywhere were welcoming and helpful, and my sincere thanks go to all those members of the clergy, church wardens, sextons and ordinary parishioners who helped me along the way and made these trips so enjoyable, and also to those who wrote to me in response to requests for information. I must also thank the Dean of St Patrick's Cathedral, the Rev. Dr Robert B. MacCarthy, whose remarks at the General Synod of 1992 on the failure to systematically photograph church buildings involved me in this work. I am also grateful to Dr Raymond Refaussé, Dr Susan Hood and the staff of the Representative Church Body Library, the staff of the Irish Architectural Archive, Dublin, and the staff of Stillorgan Library, County Dublin, all of whom were most helpful during my researches. My thanks also to Thomas J.S. Donnell of D.S.C. Partnership, Lurgan, for information on late twentieth-century Ulster churches, and to my brother-in-law Canon Richard Broadberry for reading my scripts and offering useful advice. Lastly, and most importantly, I have to thank my daughter, Linda, who did all my typing, not once but over and over again as I struggled to put my facts in order.

Finally, do look out for these cathedrals and churches as you move around the country. They are so much part of the history of Ireland and well worth a visit. You will also enjoy some of the loveliest scenery on the island.

To Linda

1. THE MIDDLE AGES

The Middle Ages, or medieval period, began with the collapse of the Roman Empire in the fifth century and lasted until roughly the middle of the fifteenth century. In England there are at least 5000 churches extant from this era but in the whole of Ireland there are less than 30 and, by a quirk of history, almost all are in the care of the Church of Ireland. We are fortunate to retain even these few following the destruction caused by the wars and unrest of the sixteenth and seventeenth centuries. By 1650, in the aftermath of the 1641 Rebellion and the Cromwellian wars, Ireland is believed to have suffered as great a devastation as Germany at the end of the Thirty Years' War.

Churches and cathedrals were frequently in the firing line. Armagh Cathedral was burnt down by Sir Phelim O'Neill in 1642. Kilkenny Cathedral suffered grievously when the city was captured by Oliver Cromwell in 1650 and lost its roof and all its stained glass. The cathedrals at Kildare, Downpatrick, Killala, Lisburn and Lismore met the same fate. In less warlike times neglect, maladministration and apathy had much the same effect. St Patrick's Cathedral, Dublin, was in such a bad state of repair in 1805 that there were plans to have it demolished and rebuilt. The situation at Dublin's Christ Church Cathedral was little better.

That the churches and cathedrals described below have survived at all is little short of a miracle, and is largely due to the generosity of wealthy private individuals in the eighteenth and nineteenth centuries and the population as a whole in the late twentieth century. Today, the future of the majority of these buildings is assured, and together they form an essential and important part of the national heritage.

The earliest existing church is St Cronan's, Tuamgraney, Co. Clare, built in the middle of the tenth century and extended eastwards two centuries later. It is a good example of the simple stone-built Irish church of the period, including the characteristic

1. (left) Clonfert Cathedral, Clonfert, Co. Galway.

2. (right) Carving of a mermaid on the chancel arch of Clonfert Cathedral.

west doorway with jambs which incline inwards and massive stone lintel. It has been in continuous use longer than any other church in Ireland and King Brian Boru, who defeated the Danes at the Battle of Clontarf in 1014, worshipped here. Further north at the monastic 'city' of Clonmacnoise in County Offaly is the eleventh-century church built by Cathal O'Connor, king of Connacht, which became St Kieran's Parish Church in 1780.

Clonfert Cathedral, in the peaceful south Galway countryside, is a simple rectangular church with a fifteenth-century tower and an interesting chancel arch. The latter includes a carving of a mermaid with comb and mirror, and it has been suggested that this is an allusion to the seafaring exploits of St Brendan the Navigator, who is buried in the grounds. The great glory of the church is the richly decorated Hiberno-Romanesque west doorway of 1167, the finest in Ireland. Each of the seven arches and the pediment is a profusion of decoration, with human and animal heads and flowers making it one of the jewels in the Irish architectural crown.

On the east bank of the River Shannon at Limerick stands St Mary's Cathedral (1180–95), founded by Donal Mór O'Brien, king of Munster, and built in the simple and plain style favoured by the Cistercians. However, a 120ft-high tower was added in the fourteenth century. Apart from Dromore Cathedral in County Down, this is the only church in Ireland with misericords or 'mercy seats', and the 23 on view, carved between 1480 and 1500, represent the only major group of Irish woodwork to survive from that time. There is a leper's squint in the north wall through which those suffering from the disease could receive communion as they were not allowed to enter a church.

Twenty miles or so upstream, and beautifully situated on the lower reaches of Lough Derg, is St Flannan's Cathedral, Killaloe, Co. Clare, founded by the same king about 1185. It is a delightful building and incorporates in the south wall an earlier and intricately decorated Hiberno-Romanesque doorway, beside which is an even earlier ogham stone with a Viking inscription. There is also a thirteenth-century font. A striking feature is the 36ft-high triple-lancet east window.

Also in County Clare is the small, simple, partially ruined Cathedral Church of St Fachan in the village of Kilfenora, which dates from the same time. Services take place in the nave, which is the only part surviving intact, having been reroofed in 1837. When Walton Empey was enthroned as bishop of Kilfenora in 1981, this was the first such event for many centuries and a new cathedra or bishop's throne was donated for the occasion.

Eastwards, in Leinster, is the charming, secluded, twelfth-century St Laserian's Cathedral, delightfully situated in a tranquil

3. St Laserian's Cathedral, Old Leighlin, Co. Carlow.

4. (left) Twelfth-century west doorway of Clonfert Cathedral, Co. Galway.

5.(right) A seventeenth-century stucco memorial at St Audoen's Church, Dublin.

rural setting at Old Leighlin, Co. Carlow. It has a fine east window by Catherine O'Brien, an eleventh-century font of black Kilkenny marble, and a four-bay sedilia. The pulpit is a memorial to John Finlay, dean of Leighlin from 1895 to 1912, who was murdered in 1921 during the Civil War.

The only medieval parish church in Dublin is St Audoen's, Cornmarket, where the twelfth-century nave is all that remains of the original building and is the present church. However, an adjoining guild chapel of St Anne has recently been reroofed and recreated as a museum dedicated to life in the Dublin of the Middle Ages. Prior to the Reformation it was the most important church in the city and supported by the guilds and rich merchants, but as the latter moved out during the eighteenth century the congregation declined. It contains a twelfth-century Norman font and two rare seventeenth-century stucco monuments on wooden frames, both in excellent condition. St Audoen is the patron saint of Rouen in Normandy.

St Mary's, Clonmel, Co. Tipperary, dates from the thirteenth century but was largely reconstructed in the fifteenth, and the west and east windows date from that time. The stained glass in the latter is by Catherine O'Brien. The nave was rebuilt and the north transept added in the nineteenth century. Externally the octagonal tower and crow-stepped gable are unusual features in an Irish church. Remnants of the town wall which saw fierce fighting during Cromwell's assault at the end of the siege in 1650 form the north and west boundaries of the churchyard. Also in County Tipperary is Holy Trinity Church, Fethard, which was given a charter by Edward III and dates from the fourteenth century. Its special attraction is the fine battlemented fifteenth-century west tower.

St Nicholas's, Adare, Co. Limerick, was at one time an Augustinian priory, founded in 1315. It fell into disrepair in the eighteenth century and was rebuilt in 1807 as the parish church incorporating the remains of the old building, which mostly dated from the fifteenth century. The lovely choir includes a three-bay sedilia, an ancient font, fine wooden stalls and magnificent stained glass. The nave contains memorials to the second and fifth earls of Dunraven, to whom we are indebted for the church we see today.

South of Malahide in County Dublin stands the interesting and unique thirteenth-century St Dolough's Church, which is built entirely of stone, including the steeply pitched roof. It adjoins the present church, built by W.H. Lynn in 1863. The tower at the west end of the ancient building includes an anchorite's cell.

St Brigid's Cathedral, Kildare, dates from the thirteenth century but has been much rebuilt, with a major and beautiful restoration completed in 1996. St Brigid, who died in 523, is, with

6. St Brigid's Cathedral, Kildare, Co. Kildare.

Patrick and Columba, one of the greatest Irish saints, and their lives are depicted in the west window. She was hugely influential in her day and a reminder that females in the church are nothing new. The nearby round tower is the second-highest in Ireland and accessible to the public.

Kilkenny is probably the most interesting inland town in Ireland and was an important centre of Norman civic and religious power. St Canice's Cathedral, in the early English Gothic style, was completed in 1285, and despite periods of decline has survived more completely than any other Irish cathedral. It has a beautifully proportioned nave and is a wonderfully serene building with much fine stained glass. It is notable for its sixteenth-century tombs and monuments and the choir stalls of 1904. Close by is a 100ft-high round tower built about 849.

There is a great variety of churches in County Cork and three of these were founded in the twelfth and thirteenth centuries. The largest and probably the most important is St Mary's Collegiate Church, Youghal, which retains its medieval character and has many interesting features, including an unusually large pulpit with a canopy of bog wood, a monument to Richard Boyle, earl of Cork, completed in 1620, and stained glass windows which depict, *inter alia*, the coat of arms of Sir Walter Raleigh, who lived for a while in the town and is credited with introducing both the potato and tobacco into Ireland — no mean feat! There is a Norman font dated *c.* 1350, whilst the splendid chancel contains a four-bay sedilia and a collection of finely carved stone heads.

About fifteen miles further west is the fourteenth-century Cathedral Church of St Colman in the village of Cloyne, the nave of which is bereft of its fittings, with only the beautiful choir now used for worship. It is associated with the eminent philosopher George Berkeley, who was dean from 1734 to 1753, and there is a fine recumbent alabaster statue to his memory in the north transept. Today the majority of ancient churches are on the tourist trail and the resultant large numbers of visitors play an important role in their upkeep. Cloyne, however, is somewhat off the beaten track and, being a large building with a small congregation, is not easy to maintain. Nevertheless, a major restoration is under way, including the reroofing of the nave. There is an ivy-clad round tower nearby. Further west again, in the same county, is St Multose's, one of the least-changed medieval parish churches. Situated in the heart of the historic and attractive coastal town of

Kinsale, it is a substantial twelfth-century building with an unusually large tower which also served as a defensive position with embrasures for use by archers. There is a font dated *c.* 1190, whilst the regimental flags of the Highland Light Infantry, carried at the Battle of Waterloo (1815), are in the chancel.

The Collegiate Church of St Nicholas, Galway, founded in 1320, is the largest medieval parish church in Ireland. It was extended during the fifteenth and sixteenth centuries by the Lynch family, whose most famous member, James Lynch, first mayor of Galway, was said to have hanged his son for murder. However, recent research suggests that this story has no basis in fact. The north transept contains a 4500-volume Victorian library, and an interesting rarity is an early sixteenth-century free-standing holy water stoup. A variety of gargoyles, including a monkey and an eagle, line the wall above the south porch. It is widely believed that Christopher Columbus worshipped here in 1477 at a time when a prosperous Galway traded extensively with Spain and the Mediterranean world.

7. Detail from the seventeenth-century memorial to Richard Boyle, earl of Cork, in St Mary's Church, Youghal, Co. Cork.

The Cathedral Church of St Patrick, Armagh, Co. Armagh, and the Cathedral Church of the Holy and Undivided Trinity, Downpatrick, Co. Down, have much in common. Both are in Ulster, both are impressively sited on a hill at the end of a long avenue rising from the town below, both have had a turbulent history, and both have strong associations with St Patrick, who ruled that Armagh should have pre-eminence over all other churches in Ireland, as indeed it has, and who is believed to be buried under a great granite slab in the cathedral grounds at Downpatrick.

There has been a church on the site of Armagh Cathedral since the fifth century, but constant plunderings and burnings led to much reconstruction over the centuries. In 1834 it was again in a state of decay, and in that year it was decided to rebuild to the enlarged design of Archbishop O'Scanlain in 1268. The architect was Lewis N. Cottingham and the result is in most respects a nineteenth-century building with remnants from the thirteenth, seventeenth and eighteenth centuries. The red sandstone exterior gives it a warm, welcoming appearance, whilst the interior contains a fine selection of monuments, the best of which is probably the recumbent figure of Dean Peter Drelincourt. Also impressive is the reredos of 1913 by Fellows Prynne. King Brian Boru is buried in the grounds.

The history of Downpatrick Cathedral parallels that of Armagh in many ways. There has been a church on the site since the fifth century, but the same pattern of destruction and rebuilding

8. The Cathedral Church of St Patrick, Armagh, Co. Armagh.

9. Corbel in the form of a head at Armagh Cathedral.

emerges and it was in ruins in 1786. An Act of Parliament in 1790 led to its reconstruction, which was helped by a grant of £1000 from King George III, the remainder of the cost being provided by leading local families, whose coats of arms are displayed on the north and south walls. Whilst it incorporates remnants from the fourteenth and fifteenth centuries, it is in large measure a Gothic Revival building with box pews of the Regency period, in the centre of which is the bishop's throne with the judge's box opposite. The fine eighteenth-century organ, also a present from King George, is sited above the choir screen. The same king presented Trinity College, Dublin, with a pipe organ which, today, is considered the most important of its kind in Ireland. It was transferred to St Fintan's, Durrow, Co. Laois, in 1842, where it is still in use.

Finally, only a few hundred yards from one another in Dublin we come to Christ Church Cathedral and St Patrick's Cathedral. It is unusual for any city to have two cathedrals for the one denomination, and one of the ironies of Irish history is that in this overwhelmingly Catholic city the only two cathedrals are

10. (right) Bust of Dean Jonathan Swift in St Patrick's Cathedral, Dublin (1766).

11. (below) Detail of memorial at St Patrick's Cathedral, Dublin, depicting the two sons of Richard Boyle, earl of Cork (seventeenth century).

12. Nave of Christ Church Cathedral, Dublin (photo courtesy of the Cathedral).

13. Madonna and Child by Imogen Stuart at Christ Church Cathedral, Dublin (twentieth century).

Protestant. Both date from the twelfth century and are essentially Early English Gothic in style. Both have suffered greatly over the years and were in very poor repair from the mid-sixteenth to the mid-nineteenth century. In the seventeenth century Christ Church had a tavern in the crypt, whilst the area between it and St Patrick's was a warren of filthy lanes and alleys occupied by squalid dwellings and miserable shops. Both were saved in the mid-nineteenth century when major works of restoration were undertaken. Sir Benjamin Lee Guinness paid the whole cost of St Patrick's, while Henry Roe did the same for Christ Church and bankrupted himself in the process.

St Patrick's is the largest Irish cathedral and the National Cathedral of the Church of Ireland, with its splendid monuments, memorials and regimental flags. History weighs heavily here, and it is forever associated with Jonathan Swift, who was dean from 1713 until his death in 1745. The organ is the largest and most powerful in the country, and the choir has sung morning and evening office daily for over 700 years. The choir school was founded in 1432.

Christ Church is a beautiful, dignified building, rich in detail and gracefully proportioned. Its twelfth-century crypt is the oldest structure in Dublin and contains a treasury which includes the magnificent gilded plate given by William of Orange after his victory at the Battle of the Boyne. The belfry contains nineteen bells, five of which date from 1738, and on the eve of the third millennium all nineteen were rung, the greatest number anywhere in the world on that eventful night. Other interesting features are the fifteenth-century brass lectern, the stocks made in 1670 and the heart of St Laurence O'Toole, brought from Normandy in 1230. The latter is the only reliquary in a Protestant church in Ireland. The Cathedral witnessed the crowning of the Pretender Lambert Simnel as Edward VI of England and France in 1487 and was the first Irish church to use the 1549 Book of Common Prayer. The choir was founded in 1493 and joined the choir of St Patrick's to sing at the first performance of Handel's 'Messiah' at the New Music Hall, Fishamble Street, Dublin, on 13 April 1742.

2. FROM THE REFORMATION TO 1700

I n 1517 Martin Luther nailed his 95 theses to the church door at Wittenberg in Germany and set in motion the great protest against the corrupt practices of the medieval papacy known as the Reformation. In 1533 King Henry VIII proclaimed himself head of the English church and the next year, after a revolt by the House of Fitzgerald, he determined to bring the entire island of Ireland under English control. This policy was followed by his daughter, Queen Elizabeth I, who also sought to convert the entire population to the reformed church order. The result was a series of devastating wars which ended with the defeat of the combined Irish and Spanish forces at the Battle of Kinsale in 1601 and the 'Flight of the Earls' to the continent of Europe in 1607.

In the early years of the Reformation the reformed order simply used the existing churches, and it was not until 1578 that the first 'Protestant' church was built on a hill overlooking Newry, Co. Down. There is still a church, St Patrick's, on this site but it bears no resemblance to the original. Another early church, deconsecrated in 1973, was Kilbrogan, Bandon, Co. Cork, built between 1610 and 1625. St John's Church, Islandmagee, Co. Antrim, dates back to 1596 and is believed to be largely original. It is a delightful building, beautifully situated overlooking Lough Larne and typical of the simple churches of the early seventeenth century, with its heavy buttresses, rectangular two- and four-light mullioned windows and small bellcote on the apex of the roof at the west end.

Another early church is Clonfeakle Parish Church, Benburb, Co. Tyrone (1618–22), which was built by Sir Richard Wingfield in the early years of the Scottish and English Plantation of Ulster and is considered to be the most perfect 'Planter's church' to survive, with its buttresses, curly label moulds and elaborate east window. It is also the oldest church in the north-west of Ireland still in regular use. There is a memorial to Captain James Hamilton who was killed at the Battle of Benburb in 1646 when the Irish under Owen Roe O'Neill defeated a Scottish army led by General Monro.

At about the same time, in 1614, when Carrickfergus, Co. Antrim, was the most important town in Ulster, St Nicholas's Church was built on the site of a twelfth-century Norman church not far from the imposing castle which continues to dominate the harbour and where William of Orange landed in 1690. It is the largest surviving seventeenth-century church and was further extended in the eighteenth century by the addition of a fine Georgian tower and steeple. Its most important interior feature is the memorial to the lord deputy of Ireland Sir Arthur Chichester (1563–1625), which is considered to be the finest seventeenth-century monument of its kind in Ireland.

Fifty-two years later, in 1666, Bishop Jeremy Taylor built Middle Church, Ballinderry, Co. Antrim. Despite restoration it is little changed from its original state, with its central oak three-decker pulpit and reader desk, box pews, stone-paved aisle and period fittings. Lit only by candlelight, there is a candlestick on each pew.

Also lit by candlelight is the delightful St Andrew's Church, Balligan, near Ballywalter, Co. Down. This is of similar construction to those already described except that there is a large porch at the west end with an outer west door. The inner door to the church is a sturdy semi-classical stone archway with the date 1704 inscribed. Despite a small congregation there is a caped choir and, as at Middle Church, long-handled pans are used for the collection.

14. St John's Church, Islandmagee, Co. Antrim (1596).

15. (left)
Candlestick on a
pew in Middle
Church,
Ballinderry, Co.
Antrim (church
— 1666).

16. (right) St
Andrew's Church,
Balligan, Co.
Down (1704).

Another church which, when first built, would have looked like the one at Ballinderry is Holy Trinity, Waringstown, Co. Down (1681), but it has been much extended since with the addition of a tower (1745), the south aisle (1859) and a chancel by Sir Thomas Drew in 1888. However, it is of great interest because the original oak roof survives together with the decorated oak pillars which have supported it for over 300 years. There are box pews and a splendid oak pulpit with sounding-board which, although not as old as the roof, matches it perfectly. This is a church full of character.

St Michael's Donaghmore Parish Church, Castlecaulfield, Co. Tyrone (1680), was built under the auspices of the Rev. George Walker, the defender of Londonderry during the great siege of 1689. The south porch, dated 1685, is an early Ulster attempt at classicism, whilst nearby is an attractive Gothic window of 1622 saved from the old church at Donaghmore which was destroyed in the 1641 Rebellion. The sundial on the tower is dated 1485. The Rev. Charles Wolfe, who was a curate here in the early nineteenth century, wrote the famous poem 'The burial of Sir John Moore', described by Lord Byron as the finest ode in the English language.

Also in County Tyrone is St Cone's, Castlederg, with tower and doorway dating from the late sixteenth or early seventeenth century. The door-case with its Tuscan columns and high open pediment is described by Alistair Rowan as 'one of the oldest as well as one of the most accomplished pieces of classicism in what was then a very remote part of the country'. There is a fine memorial in the outer south wall to a parishioner, Robert Kyle, who died in 1759.

There are two other Ulster churches which are early seventeenth-century in origin but much altered. All Saints' Church, Antrim, Co. Antrim, has windows which may date back as far as 1596, whilst there are defensive loopholes for marksmen in the north and east walls! Tomregan Parish Church, Ballyconnell, Co. Cavan, is attractively situated within earthen fortifications and was enhanced by the addition of a tower and spire in 1814. The interior contains fine plasterwork and the 'Tomregan stone', which came from a medieval church and is thought to represent the seventh-century St Bricin, who had a reputation as a surgeon.

17. Window at St Michael's Church, Castlecaulfield, Co. Tyrone (c. 1622).

*18. South
doorway at St
Cone's Church,
Castlederg, Co.
Tyrone (1635).*

The few remaining churches of the period are all in Leinster. St James's Church, Castledermot, Co. Kildare, is dated *c.* 1660. It has been much restored since. Its setting is an ancient monastic site with two fine sculptured high crosses, an isolated twelfth-century Romanesque doorway and a tenth-century castellated round tower. The latter is unusual as the entrance is at ground level, a peculiarity it shares with another round tower on Slattery Island off the coast of County Clare.

St Kevin's Church (1698) on a hillside outside the village of Hollywood, Co. Wicklow, is, from the outside, a typically simple seventeenth-century church. However, what makes it unique is that it encloses, under a layer of plaster, a continuous stone barrel-vault roof which is probably twelfth-century but may be much earlier.

St Michan's Church, Church Street, Dublin (1685–6 — Sir William Robinson), replaced an eleventh-century Norse church which for nearly six centuries was the only city parish church north of the River Liffey. During the eighteenth century it was one of the wealthiest parishes, and two interesting items remain from that period: firstly the organ installed in 1725 and rebuilt in 1952, which Handel is said to have played during rehearsals for the first performance of the 'Messiah' in 1742, and secondly the Stool of Repentance, where disgraced parishioners confessed their wrongdoings during services. The vaults are famous for their mummified bodies and also contain the death-mask of Theobald Wolfe Tone (1763–98). The burial service for Charles Stewart Parnell (1846–91) was held in this church.

There is an interesting postscript to church-building at the end of the seventeenth century following events in France. When Louis XIV revoked the Edict of Nantes in 1685, some of the considerable number of Huguenots who fled to Ireland set up a colony in Portarlington, Co. Laois, and built a church known as the 'Huguenot Church' in 1696. A French translation of the Book of Common Prayer was in use from 1715 and all services were conducted in that language until 1817. A new church, St Paul's, was

19. St James's Church, Castledermot, Co. Kildare (c. 1660).

erected in 1851 and is known as the 'French Church' to this day. There was also an 'English church' in the town but it has not survived as a church. The most prominent and wealthiest Huguenot family in Ireland was the La Touche family, and they built St Patrick's Church, Carnalway, Co. Kildare (1792), and Christ Church, Delgany, Co. Wicklow (1789), entirely at their own expense. The latter contains a striking 24ft-high monument to David La Touche, whose father fought in the Williamite army at the Battle of the Boyne in 1690.

20. Detail from the imposing memorial to David La Touche in Christ Church, Delgany, Co. Wicklow, showing one of his three sons (c. 1787).

3. CATHEDRALS OF THE SEVENTEENTH, EIGHTEENTH AND NINETEENTH CENTURIES

Eighteen of the cathedrals built during these three centuries survive and all replace earlier churches, some of which dated back to the dawn of Christianity in Ireland. Some contain fragments from the Middle Ages, but these are so few and so frequently hidden from sight that these buildings cannot claim to be of the medieval period. The possible exception is Tuam, with its great twelfth-century chancel arch, but it is essentially a nineteenth-century building.

The first cathedral built after the Reformation was the Cathedral Church of St Columb, Derry, Co. Londonderry, the foundation stone of which was laid in 1628, with work completed in 1633. It is in a style known as Planter's Gothic, and sits on the highest point within the walls of the city. A spire was added and many changes made in the nineteenth century. Much damage was caused during the siege of 1689, and it suffered again during the civil strife at the end of the twentieth century. The interior contains the largest collection of monuments of any church in Ulster and many regimental flags, including two captured from the French during the siege.

The Cathedral Church of St Carthage, pleasantly situated in Lismore, Co. Waterford, was rebuilt in 1633 by Richard Boyle, earl of Cork, around the ruins of its medieval predecessor, and was further restored by Sir William Robinson from 1679 to 1688. Its extremely elegant spire was added in 1827 by J. and G.R. Pain. The noteworthy sixteenth-century tomb of the McGrath family is in the nave.

The Cathedral Church of St Fachtna in the small village of Rosscarbery, Co. Cork, was built towards the end of the seventeenth century and incorporates some medieval remains from the church destroyed in the 1641 Rebellion. It contains an unusually large narthex or porch which is almost as long as the

*21. St Columb's
Cathedral, Derry, Co.
Londonderry (1628).*

nave, as well as a variety of memorials. The pleasing spire was erected in 1806 and there is a stained glass window in memory of Henry Becher, son of the dean, who was killed in the Great War.

The Cathedral Church of St Patrick, Killala, on the north coast of County Mayo, was also built in the latter part of the seventeenth century on the site of a church said to have been founded by St Patrick. When the French invasion force landed near here in 1798, the first person of importance their commander, General Humbert, met was the bishop of Killala. Humbert told him that he had come 'to rid Ireland of the English yoke', which wasn't good news from the bishop's point of view. However, he survived the encounter and afterwards praised the discipline and correctness of the French soldiers whilst in the town.

The Cathedral Church of St Eunan, Raphoe, Co. Donegal, is another rebuilt at the end of the seventeenth century and incorporates some fragments, including a three-seat sedilia, of a previous medieval building. The transepts were added in 1702 and the extremely tall tower in 1737. An interesting relic is the remains of a carved ninth-century door-lintel representing the Arrest in the Garden.

Christ Church Cathedral, opposite the Linen Hall in the heart of Lisburn, Co. Antrim, was rebuilt early in the eighteenth century following the loss of its predecessor by fire in 1707 and the slim octagonal spire was raised a century later. A chancel was added in the late nineteenth century, along with many other changes. There is a memorial to the Huguenot Louis Crommelin, one of the founders of the Ulster linen industry, whose grave, with other members of his family, is in the churchyard. Descendants of the Huguenot community still worship in the cathedral. There is also a fine memorial to General John Nicholson (1821–57), a hero of the Great Indian Mutiny, who was killed at the Siege of Delhi. The artist was the Dublin-born John Henry Foley (1818–74), one of the leading Victorian sculptors.

The Cathedral Church of Christ the Redeemer in Dromore, Co. Down, retains a few walls of the church built in 1661 to replace a previous church destroyed in the 1641 Rebellion. The present building mainly dates from the many extensions carried out in the nineteenth century. The person most closely associated with

22. The Cathedral of St Carthage, Lismore, Co. Waterford (1633).

23

23. St Macartan's Cathedral, Clogher, Co. Tyrone (1744).

Dromore is the seventeenth-century Bishop Jeremy Taylor, who is buried beneath the chancel and is the subject of one of the six misericords in the chapter stalls, as is the philosopher Bishop George Berkeley. Bishop Taylor wrote two famous books, *Holy living* (1650) and *Holy dying* (1651), which advocate temperance and moderation in all things. The vestments of Bishop Thomas Percy, a revered eighteenth-century cleric, are displayed in a glass-fronted wardrobe in the choir.

The Cathedral Church of St Mary the Virgin and St John the Baptist in Sligo town replaced a medieval church and was built *c.* 1731, the architect being the German-born Richard Cassels. It was remodelled in 1812 when battlements were added to the walls, and this feature and the large castellated tower give it the appearance of a small castle. However, the interior, which includes a memorial to Susan Mary Yeats, mother of the poet W.B. Yeats, is homely and inviting. It did not gain cathedral status until 1961, when it replaced the cathedral in Elphin, Co. Roscommon, which was abandoned after suffering severe damage in a storm.

The Cathedral Church of St Macartin on high ground in the

heart of Enniskillen, Co. Fermanagh, was built in 1841–2 to replace a smaller church, the architect being William Farrell. In style it is similar to the Planter's Gothic of St Columb's, Derry, and the only major change over the years was the extension of the chancel in 1889. On either side of the latter two life-size marble generals glare at one another, whilst overhead hang the colours of two famous regiments of the British Army, the Royal Inniskilling Dragoons and the Royal Inniskilling Fusiliers.

The Cathedral Church of St Patrick, Trim, Co. Meath, was only elevated to cathedral status in 1955 but was built in 1802–3, incorporating the imposing six-storey tower raised by Richard, duke of York, in 1449, when the town was of great importance with the largest castle ever built in Ireland. Further south, in the village of Ferns, Co. Wexford, is the small Cathedral Church of St Edan (built in 1816–17 with an extensive restoration in 1901), which adjoins the remains of a thirteenth-century cathedral. Ferns was at one time the capital of the king of Leinster and an important monastic and religious centre as far back as the sixth century.

The same is true of the Cathedral Church of St Mary, Tuam, Co. Galway (1861–78 — Sir Thomas Deane), built on a sixth-century monastic site and replacing a twelfth-century cathedral. The great glory of the latter was the chancel arch, one of the treasures of

24. The reredos at Christ Church Cathedral, Waterford (c. 1779).

25. St Fin Barre's Cathedral, Cork (1865–79).

Hiberno-Romanesque architecture and the widest of its kind. This has been successfully incorporated into the present building, which underwent a major restoration in 1997.

26. (left) The Foolish Virgins on the west façade of St Fin Barre's Cathedral, Cork.

The Cathedral Church of St Fethlimidh, Kilmore, Co. Cavan (1858–60 — William Slater), also known as the Bedell Memorial Church, is set on a hill in the heart of the countryside south-west of Cavan town. It is a dignified building and incorporates a fine twelfth-century Romanesque doorway which was previously part of the abbey on Trinity Island in Lough Oughter. The bishop of Kilmore from 1629 to 1642 was William Bedell, who is famous as the first person to translate the Bible into Irish. He is buried in the nearby churchyard.

27. (right) The Angel of Resurrection, St Fin Barre's Cathedral, Cork.

There are three Georgian cathedrals, two in Munster and one in Ulster. The latter is the Cathedral Church of St Macartan (1744 — James Martin), which sits on the top of a steep hill in the village of Clogher, Co. Tyrone. It is cruciform in shape, which is unusual for a Georgian church, and has a broad, pedimented west front surmounted by a robust, balustraded tower. There is a fine Venetian east window and large round-headed windows in the nave

28. Detail from the pulpit of St Fin Barre's Cathedral, Cork.

and transepts. There is also stained glass by artists associated with An Túr Gloine, whilst in the porch are portraits of all the bishops of Clogher since the sixteenth century. Peter Galloway describes this church as 'an attractive example of a classical cathedral' and Maurice Craig views it as 'a mannerly work in mid 18th century classic'. It is a lovely building in a fine state of preservation.

The foundation stone of the Cathedral Church of St John the Baptist and St Patrick's Rock, Cashel, Co. Tipperary, was laid in 1763 but the building was not completed until 25 years later. It was very controversial at the time, having replaced the twelfth-century cathedral on the Rock of Cashel which was abandoned and left roofless. The new church was a galleried four-bay structure with a three-storey porch and a two-storey tower to which a spire by Sir Richard Morrison was added in 1812. Today, externally, it is one of the most elegant of all Irish Georgian churches. The seventeenth-century communion silver from the medieval church is still in use, whilst, nearby, the library founded by Archbishop Bolton in 1730 has a fine collection of sixteenth- and seventeenth-century books. The most notable tomb in the old cathedral is that of the disreputable Bishop Myler Magrath, who changed religion as expediency required and even managed to be Church of Ireland bishop of Clogher at the same time as he was Roman Catholic bishop of Down and Connor. He married twice, had several children and died a wealthy man in 1622 at the age of 99.

Christ Church Cathedral (1779 — John Roberts) in the heart of Waterford, Co. Waterford, is the finest eighteenth-century ecclesiastical building in Ireland, with a western Doric portico, tower and spire. Inside, tall slender Corinthian columns support the ceiling with its delicate rococo stuccowork, while light floods in through the clear glass of the large round-headed windows. The stuccowork on the beautiful reredos is also of high quality. Amongst the many memorials is the macabre fifteenth-century tomb of James Rice, who was mayor of Waterford eleven times. Another commemorates the five grandsons of Colonel E. Roberts, all of whom died in the Great War. It is remarkable that John Roberts (1714–96), the architect of Christ Church, is also the architect of Waterford Roman Catholic cathedral and is believed to be the only European architect ever to build two cathedrals in the one city. He had 21 children, and Field Marshal Frederick Roberts V.C. of Boer War fame was a great-grandson. A medieval cathedral (a scale model of which is on view) was demolished to make way for the new church and it was in that building that the most famous (or infamous) wedding in Irish history took place in 1170 between the Norman Strongbow, earl of Pembroke, and Aoife, daughter of Dermot MacMurrough, king of Leinster.

Without doubt, the finest building ever erected by the Church of Ireland and a truly splendid church is St Fin Barre's Cathedral in Cork city (1865–79 — William Burges). It is in the French Gothic style of the early thirteenth century, which, with its three spires, gives it a Continental and rather alien appearance. The tallest of the spires rises to 240ft, which is nearly 100ft more than the length of the cathedral, making it rather compressed. The entire structure is, nevertheless, beautifully proportioned. A charming feature is the golden Angel of Resurrection with her trumpets at the apex of the chancel roof. The interior is equally fine, with elaborate carving, a lovely rose west window, a richly decorated sanctuary roof, a wide and imposing pulpit, a 9ft-high solid brass lectern and, most striking of all, the bishop's throne, which is over 40ft tall. St Fin Barre's has been described by Maurice Craig as 'one of the wonders of Ireland' and by Peter Galloway as 'one of the most remarkable sights in Ireland'. A major restoration is under way which should keep this national treasure safe until well into the twenty-first century.

The last great building project undertaken by the Church of Ireland was the Cathedral Church of St Anne, Belfast, where work began in 1899 but was not completed until 82 years later in 1981. It was built on the site of an imposing Georgian church with the

29. The huge Celtic cross on the north transept of St Anne's Cathedral, Belfast.

same name which continued in use for three years until completely engulfed by its replacement. Eight architects were involved, the first being Sir Thomas Drew and the last Robert McKinstry. It is in the Romanesque style, with a most dignified nave completed in 1910. Thereafter work was done in fits and starts, but the overall effect is spacious and harmonious. The leader of the Ulster Unionist Party from 1911 to 1922, Lord Edward Carson, is buried in the south aisle, but today St Anne's in its Chapel of Unity works hard for peace and reconciliation in Belfast and the rest of Ireland. Possibly the most striking feature of the cathedral is the enormous Celtic cross on the exterior of the north transept. It is an extraordinary sight.

30. (above) The font of St Anne's Cathedral, Belfast.

31. (right) Memorial to the men of the 36th (Ulster) Division who died in the Great War at St Anne's Cathedral, Belfast.

4. THE GEORGIAN CHURCH

The victories of King William of Orange at the Boyne (1690) and Aughrim (1691) finally consolidated English rule in Ireland, and over the next 100 years a gradual transformation took place in the generally peaceful climate which prevailed. Towns were rebuilt, fine houses erected throughout the land, and impressive engineering projects initiated. The greatest change was in Dublin, where streets were widened, great public buildings erected and splendid squares created, all of which led to its becoming the second city of the English-speaking world in the eighteenth century. This was also the age of the Grand Tour, when wealthy young men spent long periods in Europe to complete their education. Many discovered the architectural glories of ancient Greece and Rome and returned home determined to build their houses and important buildings on classical lines. The fashion extended to churches and was a popular style in Irish cities and towns during the reigns of George I to George IV (1714 to 1830). However, with few exceptions, it had little impact in rural areas.

During the seventeenth and eighteenth centuries the main emphasis was on the preacher, and worshippers were referred to as auditors. The auditory church was perfected by Sir Christopher Wren, who postulated that 'in our reformed religion it should seem vain to make a parish church larger than that all who are present can both hear and see'. The simple churches of the seventeenth and early eighteenth centuries fulfilled this role to perfection, and the Georgian or Classical church was similarly inspired but on a grander scale. The typical church was box-shaped, with large round-headed clear glass windows and a handsome west front with a central tower and spire. Internally it had galleries on three sides, box pews and a shallow sanctuary with the pulpit in a prominent position. The decoration, especially the stuccowork, was often of a high standard. Classical columns and pilasters were a common feature.

One of the earliest, dating from 1700, is St Thomas's Parish

Church overlooking the sea at Wicklow, Co. Wicklow. The three-sided gallery is one of the first in an Irish church, and it has a four-storey tower and unusual cupola raised by the Eaton family in 1770. Their crest can be seen on the weather-vane — a lion bearing a sheaf of straw. In the south wall is an attractive oculus and a stained glass window which shows the church as it was prior to the addition of the chancel in 1912, whilst in the south porch is a Hiberno-Romanesque doorway rescued from a medieval church which once occupied the same site. One of the parishioners was Captain Robert Halpin, commander of the *Great Eastern*, which laid the first transatlantic cable in 1866, and there are memorials to him in the church and the town.

St Mary's Church, Mary Street, Dublin, is believed to have been built to the designs of Sir William Robinson about 1701 but has also been attributed to Thomas Burgh. It was the earliest galleried church in the city, with an interesting east window of baroque design, a splendid reredos and an organ built *c*. 1700 by the famous organ-maker Renatus Harris. This organ in its richly carved wooden case was one of the oldest in Ireland. It was here

32. St Thomas's Church, Wicklow, Co. Wicklow (c. 1700).

33. War memorial stained glass window at St Thomas's Church, Wicklow, Co. Wicklow, depicting the church prior to the addition of the chancel.

that John Wesley preached his first Irish sermon in 1747 and where Lord Charlemont (1728–99), Richard Brinsley Sheridan (1751–1816), Theobald Wolfe Tone (1763–9) and Seán O'Casey (1880–1964) were baptised. It was also where Sir Benjamin Lee Guinness, the saviour of St Patrick's Cathedral, was married. This historic church was deconsecrated in 1986, following which its interior was gutted and the reredos, organ, box pews and other artefacts removed. The contents of the crypts were reinterred in the vaults of St Michan's Church. The building has since been used as a retail outlet but plans are afoot to 'restore' it as a super-pub capable of accommodating up to two thousand people!

Another galleried church is St Ann's, Dawson Street, Dublin (1720 — Isaac Wills), which was built in what was then a fashionable suburb and whose parishioners later included Theobald Wolfe Tone and Bram Stoker (1847–1912). The interior has not greatly changed except that the original clear glass windows were replaced in Victorian times by stained glass, including three by Wilhelmina Geddes. The west front was rebuilt in 1868 in the neo-Romanesque style by Sir Thomas Deane, but the planned massive belfry was never completed. A charity was established in 1723 to provide bread for the poor and continues today with the bread shelf in the choir. Amongst the memorials is one to Sir Hugh Lane (1875–1915).

The interior of St Werburgh's (1715 — Thomas Burgh),

Werburgh Street, Dublin, is a veritable 'time capsule' of the Georgian church with every original feature intact, including the organ which has never been rebuilt. For many years the lord lieutenant sat in his special pew in the middle of the west gallery, where the royal coat of arms can still be seen. Almost directly opposite is the magnificent wooden pulpit designed by Francis Johnston and carved by Richard Stewart, whilst nearby in the aisle is the font used at the christening of Jonathan Swift (1667–1745) and the composer John Field (1782–1837). The church originally had a tower and spire, but after the 1803 Rebellion it was feared that they posed a security risk to Dublin Castle and they were removed. Lord Edward Fitzgerald, the leader of the 1798 Rebellion, is buried in the vaults. His aunt, Lady Louisa Connolly, was the only mourner at his interment.

St Catherine's, Thomas Street, Dublin (1758 — John Smyth), is granite-built with what Maurice Craig has described as 'the finest façade of any church in Dublin being a superbly virile composition in Roman Doric'. It was deconsecrated in 1967 owing to

34. St Werburgh's Church, Werburgh St., Dublin (1715).

35. The font in St Werburgh's Church, Dublin (seventeenth century).

36. Detail of the pulpit designed by Francis Johnston at St Werburgh's Church, Dublin.

population decline and was soon in such a poor condition that its eventual destruction seemed inevitable. Happily, CORE (City Outreach for Renewal and Evangelism), an evangelical wing of the Church of Ireland, undertook the task of restoration in 1997 and it stands today much as it must have looked when first built. Robert Emmet (1778–1803), a member of the Church of Ireland, was executed outside this building in 1803 for his part in the abortive rebellion of the same year.

One of the best-known buildings in the city of Cork is St Ann's, Shandon (1726 — possibly John Coltsman), with a graceful west tower to which was added, about 1749, an elegant graduated turret containing a set of bells for which the church is famous and which are celebrated in the lines:

> ' 'Tis the bells of Shandon,
> That sound so grand on
> The pleasant waters of the River Lee'.

There is a splendid weather-vane in the form of a salmon 11ft long over the belfry.

37. The south door of St Patrick's Church, Donabate, Co. Dublin.

*38. (left)
Sixteenth-century
tomb-slab of
Edward Golding
and his wife in
the grounds of St
Peter's Church,
Drogheda, Co.
Louth.*

*39. (right) St
Peter's Church,
Drogheda, Co.
Louth (1748).*

The lovely little church of St Patrick's, Donabate, Co. Dublin (1758), was built under the auspices of Archbishop Charles Cobbe, who arranged that the gallery at the west end should be for the sole use of his family. This area has a fine rococo plasterwork ceiling incorporating swans, and there are benches all around so that some of the family had their backs to the preacher throughout the service! To ensure that they were comfortable in cold weather there is a fireplace in the north-west corner. This same archbishop had a cross removed from the small spire which at one time adorned the tower of St Audoen's in Dublin city, bringing the following riposte from Dean Swift:

'Christ's cross from God's house,
Cursed Cobbe has pulled down
And put in its place
What he worships — the Crown'.

Another church with a private gallery and fireplace is the cream-coloured cruciform-shaped Church of the Resurrection,

Blarney, Co. Cork (1776), which overlooks the town square and has a Venetian south window and a neo-classical interior. The gallery was for the use of the Jeffreys family of Blarney Castle, where services were held prior to the building of the church.

St Peter's, Drogheda, Co. Louth (1752 — Hugh Darley), has been described by the architectural historian Christine Casey as 'probably the finest provincial Georgian church in Ireland'. The west front is a handsome Palladian design, with a central tower and spire added by Francis Johnston 40 years later. Inside there are galleries around three sides and impressive wall monuments, while the stuccowork in the chancel is of the highest quality, as is much of the woodwork. Much damage was done to the interior following an arson attack in 1999 but it has since been restored to its former glory and is in use again for worship and as a venue for concerts and recitals. Embedded in an outer wall of the churchyard is the remarkable macabre sixteenth-century tomb-slab of Edward Golding and his wife.

40. Knockbreda parish church, Newtownbreda, Belfast (1737).

41. (above left) Moira Parish Church, Moira, Co. Down (1723).

42. (above right) West doorway of Holy Trinity Church, Ballycastle, Co. Antrim (1756).

St George's, High Street, Belfast (1816 — John Bowden), has been beautifully restored following fifteen bomb attacks and is another galleried church with a hammerbeam roof and a chancel added in 1882 with murals by Alexander Gibbs. Its outstanding feature is the splendid portico and pediment, which was once part of Ballyscullion House in County Londonderry. Brought to the city via the River Bann and Lough Neagh, these were the largest structures transported by inland waterways in Ireland up to that time.

Another church to suffer grievously from civil strife in the twentieth century was Christ Church, College Square North, Belfast (1833 — William Farrell). The second-oldest in the city, this was a fine galleried church with a Greek Revival stone Ionic front. Despite thirteen bomb and arson attacks it continued in use until 1993, when it finally succumbed following extensive damage to the roof. Although it will no longer continue as a church it has been acquired by the Royal Belfast Academical Institution, which plans to restore it as a new technology educational centre. Also still intact and in a safe new home is the unique and beautiful double-decker wooden pulpit of 1878 which somehow survived.

Knockbreda Parish Church, Church Road, Newtownbreda (1737 — Richard Cassels), is situated on a hill in south Belfast and there is a splendid view of the city from the churchyard. The latter contains a varied collection of eighteenth-century monuments, the finest of which is the Greg Memorial of *c.* 1796. The church was described in 1744 as 'a building the neatest and most complete perhaps of this kind in the Kingdom' and it is little changed since. Two other Ulster churches share many of the features of Knockbreda, with its pleasing three-bay west façade, pedimented door and central tower with octagonal spire. These are Moira Parish Church, Moira, Co. Down (1723), and Holy Trinity Church, Ballycastle, Co. Antrim (1756), each described by Maurice Craig as 'a respectable piece of classicism'. The exterior of the Ballycastle church is, however, more decorative, with a porch inscribed 'Fear God Honour the King' and a Venetian window below the balustraded tower. It was built at the sole expense of Colonel Hugh Boyd, an enterprising local landlord who did much to develop the

43. *The sanctuary of St Iberius's Church, Wexford (1775).*

44. Clondehorkey Parish Church, Ballymore, Co. Donegal (1752).

45. Interior of Clondehorkey Parish Church, Ballymore, Co. Donegal, with Venetian east window (1752).

46. St Peter's Church, Portlaoise, Co. Laois (1803).

town, and it is believed that the first service in the new church was his funeral! An attractive internal feature is the repetition of the pedimented west door on the inside.

St Iberius's Church in the main street of Wexford is sited where St Ibar founded an oratory in the sixth century. It was built in 1776, the architect being John Roberts, and replaced a number of previous churches, the last of which was erected about 1660. Broader than it is long, with a lovely sanctuary fronted by three arches resting on splendid Corinthian columns, it is decorated in a delightful Wedgwood blue with fine examples of eighteenth-century stuccowork. A gallery runs around three of the sides and there is a fine array of wall monuments. The altar rail came from St George's Church, Dublin, when the latter was deconsecrated, and the pulpit is a memorial to parishioners who died in the Great War and Second World War. Oscar Wilde's mother, Lady Jane Wilde (1821–96), was the granddaughter of Archdeacon John Elgee who was rector of St Iberius's from 1795 to 1823. She recounted how her grandfather was nearly murdered at the time of the 1798 Rebellion when a group of insurgents on the rampage in Wexford town came upon him. However, one of the mob reminded them that the rector had once done a great kindness to his family and, as a result, his life was spared and his house unharmed.

St John's, Clondehorkey Parish Church, Ballymore, near Port na Blagh, Co. Donegal (1752 — probably Michael Priestly), is one of the few Georgian country churches and is noteworthy for its Venetian east window and its south windows with Gibbs surrounds. The bellcote and vestibule, which also includes a small Venetian window, were added by Joseph Welland in 1853. Internally, the huge Venetian window fills the east wall and floods the church with light, while some eighteenth-century box pews remain *in situ* at the west end. This is a charming rural church.

The only other notable Georgian country church is St John's, Coolbanagher, Co. Laois (1785 — James Gandon), which is little changed externally. The interior, by contrast, was much altered in the nineteenth century and, although still attractive, does not have the elegance to be seen in a print attributed to James Malton soon after it was built. James Gandon (1743–1823) was the greatest resident architect of the period and designed the Custom House and the Four Courts, Dublin's finest buildings. He also designed the spire and west end of St Peter's, Portlaoise, Co. Laois (1803–5), his only other known church work in Ireland.

47. Detail from the interior of the chapel of the Rotunda Hospital, Dublin (1756).

The most splendid and expensive church built in Dublin in the early nineteenth century was St George's, Hardwicke Place (1814 — Francis Johnston). It is broader than it is long and superbly sited with an Ionic portico, a tiered tower and Wren-type spire reaching to a height of 200ft. In its early days it was a most fashionable church, and is long believed to have been where Sir Arthur Wellesley (later the Great Duke of Wellington) married Miss Kitty Pakenham. In fact, the wedding took place in the Longford family town house in Rutland (now Parnell) Square but was registered in St George's. Sadly, the church is now deconsecrated and in an unsafe condition, with the original interior gutted, the contents dispersed and its future uncertain. Despite its reduced status and the drabness of its immediate surroundings, it maintains a wonderful dignified presence and remains a prominent landmark in north Dublin. The demise of this celebrated church has had one happy outcome in that the set of eight peal bells, presented by Francis Johnston in 1828, has been re-erected in Christ Church, Taney, Co. Dublin (1818), where, for the first time in many years, they rang out again at midnight on the eve of the third millennium.

48. St Stephen's Church, Upper Mount Street, Dublin (1825).

49. Archbishop Robinson's Chapel, Armagh city (1785).

On the south side of the River Liffey, St Stephen's (the Pepper Pot Church), Upper Mount Street (1825 — John Bowden), was built in the neo-Grecian style. It also is delightfully sited and, seen from Merrion Square, is the finest vista in Dublin. The funeral service of Jack B. Yeats (1871–1957), the greatest Irish painter of the twentieth century, took place here.

Two notable Dublin eighteenth-century chapels (both now multidenominational) are the Chapel of Trinity College (1798 — Sir William Chambers) and the Chapel of the Rotunda Hospital (1756 — Richard Cassels), both of which have splendid plasterwork by Michael Stapleton and Bartholomew Cramillion respectively. The work of the latter is especially outstanding, with a wonderful ceiling of rococo plaster figures representing Faith, Hope and Charity interspersed with angels and cherubs.

While not strictly Georgian, Dublin's first great classical building, the seventeenth-century Royal Hospital, Kilmainham, incorporates a fine chapel, now deconsecrated, with magnificent carved woodwork by the Huguenot James Tabary. The ceiling, which had to be replaced in 1902, is a papier-mâché replica of the original and a rarity in Ireland. The chapel never had an organ as all services for the old soldiers were accompanied by a military band. It is currently in use as a concert and recital venue.

The chapel of Wilson's Hospital, Multyfarnham, Co. Westmeath, was built by John Pentland in 1759, the same year as the school, and has been in continuous use ever since. The main body of the church is the usual rectangle with a balustraded gallery on three sides supported by Doric columns, while the apsidal sanctuary includes three large round-headed windows with abstract stained glass. The eleven wardens who served from 1761 to 1993 are remembered by their initials on tiles in the aisle. A major restoration in 2000 included the replacement of the original seating by new pews and the erection of a circular staircase to the gallery, but these changes do not affect the overall harmony of this rare mid-Georgian building. Two memorials record the remarkable fact that more than 200 old boys of this small school served in the Great War and Second World War, of whom 40 made the supreme sacrifice.

The Blue Coat School, Blackhall Place, Dublin (later the King's Hospital) was designed by Thomas Ivory in 1772 but not completed until 1783. It includes a chapel in the north wing which, although less decorative than planned, is an elegant building lit by ten large round-headed clear glass windows with a balustraded gallery at the west end, underneath which is a pedimented doorway with Ionic pillars. There is a fine cornice at the east end, below which is a stained glass window by Evie Hone framed by twin Corinthian pilasters. The church was an important part of school life for nearly 200 years, with daily morning services and a robed choir on Sunday. One of the duties of the latter was to sing in nearby St Michan's Church each year at the service which marked the opening of the new law term. It was fitting, therefore, when the school moved to Palmerstown, Co. Dublin, in 1968, that the new owners should be the Incorporated Law Society of Ireland, who now use the deconsecrated chapel for seminars and as a banqueting hall.

Finally, close by the building in the city of Armagh which was once the primate's palace and is now occupied as a local government office, there is a church which epitomises all that was most graceful and elegant in the eighteenth century. This is the small private chapel, now deconsecrated, built for the primate, Archbishop Robinson, in 1781 by Thomas Cooley with an interior completed by Francis Johnston in 1785. It is fronted by a handsome pedimented portico supported by four Ionic columns, and internally has been described as 'one of the most beautiful surviving 18th century interiors in Ireland'. It contains a delightful bow-fronted musicians' gallery, whilst the archbishop's oaken throne and the clergy stalls are of the highest quality. The last two decades of the century were the high point of the Protestant Ascendancy, and the primate, as head of the established church, was the most powerful man in Ireland after the lord lieutenant. The primacy of the church as well as its architecture would change dramatically in the nineteenth century.

5. NON-CLASSICAL EIGHTEENTH-CENTURY CHURCHES

While the eighteenth century is synonymous with the Georgian period and the Classical church, most churches, especially in the countryside, were little different from the simple rectangular seventeenth-century churches; surviving examples are St Michael's, Aghold, Co. Wicklow (1716), Duneane Church, Duneane, Co. Antrim (1729), Bright Parish Church, near Killough, Co. Down (1745), and St Mogue's, Timogue, Co. Laois (1736). The latter is most interesting, with box pews, an aisle paved with early eighteenth-century tombstones, and a twelfth-century font with a carved head of Christ. However, the outstanding and rare feature is the pulpit flanked by the boxed lectern and clerk's desk against the east wall, with the holy table in front and the whole enclosed by a bow-shaped communion rail. There was a previous thatched church, built in 1620, on the same site which is believed to be the burial place of the many local people who died of plague in the

50. St Michael's Church, Aghold, Co. Wicklow (1716).

51. 'Three-decker' pulpit, reading desk and clerk's desk at St Mogue's Church, Timogue, Co. Laois (1736).

thirteenth and fourteenth centuries. A beautiful silver chalice of 1628 is still in use.

Tibohine Parish Church, Frenchpark, Co. Roscommon (1740), is, today, part church and part museum to the memory of Dr Douglas Hyde (1860–1949), first president of the Irish Free State and one of the seven co-founders of the Gaelic League. His father was a rector of this church and they are buried side by side in the churchyard. Another president and member of the Church of Ireland, Erskine Childers (1905–74), is buried in the churchyard of the ruined Derrylossary Church, Co. Wicklow (1820).

St Finian's, Newcastle Lyons, Co. Dublin, was built in 1724 on the site of an ancient church and incorporates a decorated Gothic fifteenth-century east window. A watercolour of *c.* 1775 by Gabriel Beranger shows that the former chancel (now disused and roofless) was thatched. The west tower is also fifteenth-century and served as a priest's residence, a feature shared by St Mary's, Leixlip, Co. Kildare (1806), another church with medieval origins.

Two churches from the period have literary connections. St John's, Edgeworthstown, Co. Longford (1716), is the church where the father of the novelist Maria Edgeworth (1767–1849) was rector, and she is buried in the grounds alongside a sister of Oscar Wilde. A later novelist, Elizabeth Bowen (1899–1973), is buried opposite St Colman's Church, Farahy, Co. Cork (1721), which holds an annual memorial service in her honour. Adjoining this church is a quaint little charity school built in the same year.

St Carthage's on the sixth-century monastic site of Rahan, Co.

52. *(above) Stained glass window of St Carthage signed 'The gift of a wayfarer 1912' in St Carthage's Church, Rahan, Co. Offaly.*

53. *(above right) A capital on the twelfth-century chancel arch at St Carthage's Church, Rahan, Co. Offaly.*

54. *(right) The east end of St Carthage's Church, Rahan, Co. Offaly, which was rebuilt in 1732. The window below the ancient wheel window was restored in the nineteenth century.*

Offaly (rebuilt 1732), is an intriguing small church which incorporates a carved early twelfth-century chancel arch with capitals in the form of human heads. Above the Romanesque east window of similar date is an earlier and rare wheel window, and on each side of the chancel is a deep recess in the wall where a priest could find privacy and quiet. There is a small but very beautiful stained glass window of St Carthage signed 'The Gift of a Wayfarer 1912'.

St Anne's, Castlemartyr, Co. Cork (1731), replaced the old parish church of 1549 destroyed in the 1641 Rebellion, while St Lachtan's, Freshford, Co. Kilkenny (1730), incorporates a fine twelfth-century Hiberno-Romanesque doorway in its western gable.

Although St Nicholas's Church, Dundalk, Co. Louth, was founded in the thirteenth century, it was substantially rebuilt in 1707 following extensive damage during both the Cromwellian and Williamite wars. It retains its heavily buttressed fourteenth-century tower to which Francis Johnston added a spire, but the latter was subsequently replaced by the present green copper spire in 1933. There are some fifteenth-century windows in the nave, which is largely eighteenth-century, and there are good monuments in the graveyard, where Agnes Burns, a sister of the Scottish poet Robert Burns, is buried.

St Nahi's, Dundrum, Co. Dublin (1760), is a mere 100m from the clamour of Dundrum Shopping Centre but retains the atmosphere of a country church. This unassuming building contains stained glass by Evie Hone and Catherine O'Brien in addition to fine needlework by Susan and Elizabeth Yeats, both buried in the churchyard and sisters of the poet W.B. Yeats. The font (previously in St Peter's, Dublin) is the one used at the baptism of the Great Duke of Wellington in 1769.

Creggan Parish Church, near Crossmaglen, Co. Armagh (1758), is situated close to the border in one of the districts most troubled by the civil unrest of the last 30 years of the twentieth century. However, against all the odds and with the benefit of grants totalling more than £600,000, it has been completely restored, along with its organ and nearby buildings. The latter include the Eastwood family vault, which some scholars believe may be a fifth-century stone church.

Christ Church, Castlebar, Co. Mayo (1739 — Richard Cassels), built on a prominent site near the town centre, was badly damaged in 1798 during the Napoleonic wars when used as a defensive position by the local militia against the invading French. This battle, popularly known as 'The Races of Castlebar', and its aftermath so demoralised the local congregation that the work to restore the church to its present appearance took 30 years and was not completed until 1829. Richard Cassels (*c.* 1690–1751), also known as Richard Castle, was born in Germany but settled in Ireland and became one of the country's most important architects. His many notable buildings include Carton House, Co. Kildare; Russborough House, Co. Wicklow; Westport House, Co. Mayo; and the Rotunda Hospital, Dublin.

During the middle of the century there was a renewed interest in Gothic architecture, and this is exemplified by St Malachi's, Hillsborough, Co. Down (1760–73), with its imposing west tower and spire rising to 210ft flanked by twin towers over each transept. Maurice Craig describes it as 'having initiated the Gothic Revival in Ireland'. This lovely church has scarcely changed since it was built and contains many notable features, including elevated

*55. St Malachi's
Church, Hillsborough,
Co. Down (1760).*

56. The elevated north transept at St Malachi's Church, Hillsborough, Co. Down
(photo courtesy of St Malachi's Church).

57.
Ballymakenny
Church, Co.
Louth (1793).

58. St Ann's
Church,
Tullaghobegly,
Co. Donegal
(1792).

59. Inch Parish Church, near Downpatrick, Co. Down (1730 — tower 1828).

60. Box pews and stove in Kilmore Parish Church, rebuilt at the Ulster Folk Museum, Cultra, Co. Down (1792).

transepts, high box pews, an organ of 1773 by John Snetzler of Bavaria, a pulpit with sounding-board, and an east window of painted glass designed by Sir Joshua Reynolds (1723–92). William Harty, father of the composer Sir Hamilton Harty, was the organist for many years. On display is a rare 1685 copy of the first Irish translation of the Bible by Bishop Bedell of Kilmore, Co. Cavan. We do not know the architect of St Malachi's but Simon Walker names no fewer than seven suspects, his preference being John Lilly of Dublin.

Two other Ulster churches in an early Gothic Revival style are Cappagh Parish Church, Mountjoy Forest, Co. Tyrone (1768), which is beautifully situated and was built at the sole expense of the rector, Dr Gibson, and Tamlaght Finlagan Parish Church, Ballykelly, Co. Londonderry (1795 — Michael Shanahan). Both have attractive towers and elegant spires, with the unusual feature of a ladder stretching the full height of the tower in the Ballykelly church. The latter also contains interesting memorials, including an elaborate early eighteenth-century wall monument to Mrs Jane Hamilton and another to a seventeen-year-old midshipman, James D. Beresford, who died when he fell from the yard-arm of the frigate *Phenix* in pursuit of the enemy in the winter of 1807.

As the eighteenth century progressed and the Protestant population increased, more churches were required. One of the loveliest is Ballymakenny, Co. Louth (1785–93), where the architect was Francis Johnston to designs of Thomas Cooley. The coat of arms of Archbishop Robinson can still be seen over the west door as a reminder of former glories because, sadly, this fine church, whilst still in good order, is deconsecrated. Francis Johnston (1760–1829) was one of the greatest of Irish-born architects, and though best known for his neo-classical work he also built the splendid Gothic Revival Chapel Royal in Dublin Castle. His hobby was bell-ringing and he had a set of twelve bells in a tower in his garden, eight of which were installed in the church of St Philip and St James, Holywood, Co. Down (1844), after his death. He was also the architect of some great public works, his most famous building being the General Post Office, Dublin (1814).

Johnston had served his apprenticeship under another eminent architect, Thomas Cooley (1740–84), who designed many churches for Archbishop Robinson, one of which, St John's, Lisnadill, Co. Armagh (1772), is especially interesting because it survives unchanged from the time of its erection. It has a tall, elegant square tower with the archbishop's coat of arms over the entrance, and inside there is a windowless east wall with a reredos on which is printed the Lord's Prayer, the Creed and the Ten Commandments. This was a common feature of eighteenth-century churches.

Other worthy examples of non-classical churches are Manorhamilton Parish Church, Manorhamilton, Co. Leitrim (1783); St Mary's, Castlecomer, Co. Kilkenny (1757 — enlarged 1818); St Finbarr's, Carrickmacross, Co. Monaghan (1779); St Mary's, Templemore, Co. Tipperary (1790); All Saints', Kilmalooda, Co. Cork (1793); and Ashfield Church, near Cootehill, Co. Cavan (1796). Four smaller but charming churches are Rathsaran, near Rathdowney, Co. Laois (1797); St John's Church, Nurney, Co. Carlow (1791); St Ann's, Tullaghobegly, Co. Donegal (1792); and Inch Parish Church, near Downpatrick, Co. Down (1730 — enlarged 1828).

Kilmore Parish Church, Crossgar, Co. Down (1792), is no longer at Crossgar but has been moved, stone by stone, to the Ulster Folk Museum, Cultra, Co. Down, where it stands as a splendid example of a late eighteenth-century church, complete with box pews and a large stove in the middle of the aisle with a flue that rises to the ceiling. It has a counterpart in the south, where a nineteenth-century church previously at Congor, Co. Tipperary, has been moved in a similar manner to the Folk Park at Bunratty, Co. Clare.

6. EARLY NINETEENTH-CENTURY 'BOARD OF FIRST FRUITS' CHURCHES

In the aftermath of the disastrous 1798 Rebellion, and to the dismay of many members of the church, the Act of Union of 1801 abolished Grattan's Parliament (1782–1800) and Ireland became a part of the United Kingdom. As if to compensate, and there were certainly political motives, there commenced an unprecedented church-building boom which lasted for 30 years and covered every part of the island, including wild and not easily accessible places such as Rathlin Island off the north Antrim coast and Inishmore on the then very remote Aran Islands. Amazingly, much of this building took place between 1800 and 1815, when Great Britain was engaged in a life-and-death struggle with Napoleon.

All of this work was controlled by a previously existing government department known as the 'Board of First Fruits' which had been established in 1711 and continued to exist until 1833, when it was superseded by the Ecclesiastical Commissioners. Prior to 1777 the revenue of the Board was meagre, but in that year Parliament voted an annual sum which enabled it to make grants (also known as gifts) for new buildings and repair. With the Act of Union, the church lost its clerical boroughs and was paid compensation in the region of £47,000, which eventually passed to the Board's funds. In addition, the Board received £5000 annually from the Government, increasing to £60,000 a year from 1810 to 1816. Between 1800 and 1823 over one million pounds, an enormous sum of money in those days, passed through its hands.

The typical grant was £500, and as many parishes could not afford much more a simple type of church became the standard and created a style which came to be known as 'First Fruits Gothic'. These were small, sturdy, unassuming buildings with a square west tower and pinnacles, a plain rectangular hall with pointed windows and a shallow sanctuary. Many had no windows in the north wall and included high box pews as a means of keeping the congregation warm during the severe winters which were common at that time. As one wit remarked, 'many were cold but few were frozen'. Between 1808 and 1829 more than 600 churches were built by gift alone and these, described as 'spiky little churches of desiccated Gothic', typified the country church which is still widespread today. One of them, Donaghmore Parish Church, Co. Laois (1801), has the cost (sterling £520) engraved on a plaque over the entrance.

Wealthy parishes were expected to fund a church from their own resources, and some did, but more often than not the cost was made up of a grant and long-term loan from the Board, with the balance paid by the parishioners and/or a local benefactor. Holy Trinity Church, Drumsallan, Eglish, Co. Armagh (1821), is a classic example of a 'First Fruits' church and cost £1790-16-0½, made up as follows:

Loan from the Board	£923.1.5½
Subscriptions	£532.0.9
Sale of materials of old church	£23.6.8½
Donation from the primate	£312.7.1½

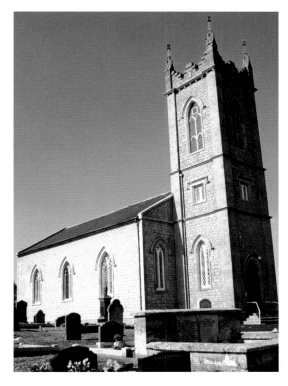

61. Holy Trinity Church, Drumsallan, Co. Armagh (1821).

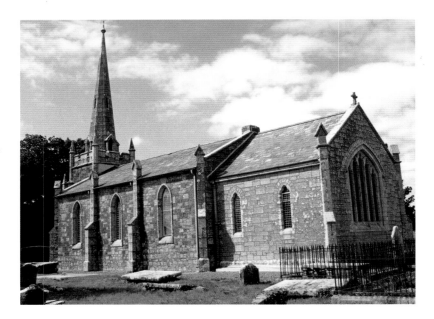

62. Staplestown Church, Co. Carlow (1821).

The addition of a spire was always desirable and greatly enhanced the status and appearance of a church but was expensive and required a wealthy congregation or local benefactor. The spires of the period were often elegant, and prime examples can be seen at St George's, Mitchelstown, Co. Cork (1804), Ballinderry Parish Church, Ballinderry, Co. Antrim (1824), St Kieran's, Cloughjordan, Co. Tipperary (1837 — J. and G.R. Pain), Staplestown, Co. Carlow (1821), and Carrigaline, Co. Cork (1828 — J. and G.R. Pain).

63. St Patrick's Church, Armoy, Co. Antrim (1820).

It was the policy of the Board to site a church in as prominent a position as possible so that nobody could be in any doubt about the power and prestige of the established church. Planners and architects of the time were experts in this respect and many country churches are beautifully situated, often on or close to old monastic sites, with St Patrick's, Armoy, Co. Antrim (1820), and the remains of its tenth-century round tower a typical example. When this happened a previous church would usually be demolished or abandoned, and some worthy buildings may well have been lost as a result. New places of worship were also built in the ruins of medieval churches, as at New Ross, Co. Wexford, where the nave of the roofless St Mary's Abbey Church was demolished and a new galleried church with a three-storey tower was built in its place about 1811, with a spire added in 1870. The architect may have been John Robertson, who rebuilt the nearby Tholsel in 1806. The old abbey was one of the largest and grandest early thirteenth-century town churches in Ireland and even today, with only the walls of the chancel and transepts still standing, is an impressive sight.

64. St Sinian's Church, Tyrrelspass, Co. Westmeath (1832).

Those churches in small towns and villages frequently occupy a focal point and add greatly to the character of the locality. An excellent example is St Tighernagh's, Clones, Co. Monaghan (1822), which dominates the attractive market-place, as does Rathdowney Parish Church, Rathdowney, Co. Laois (1818), and St Sinian's, Tyrrelspass, Co. Westmeath (1832), overlooking the village green. Another church which is visible for miles around is the attractive whitewashed Ballintoy Parish Church, Ballintoy (1812), on the north Antrim coast.

Patrick and Maura Shaffrey's description of the typical country church is very apt:

'The Church of Ireland country church and its immediate setting is among the most pleasant features in country districts. The simple lines of the building, its walls of grey stone, the elegant spire reaching to the sky, the mature trees, the graveyard, all create a sense of timelessness and tranquillity'.

Kevin Myers writes in a similar vein:

'The churches of the Church of Ireland are among the great uncelebrated treasures of the Irish countryside. What civilised heart does not surge an extra beat at the sight of the spire rising above a stand of beech in the middle of nowhere, and at the thought of the small congregation of farmers and traders converging down sinuous bohereens on cold Sundays?'

Although most 'First Fruits' churches are simple and unadorned, there are others which had attention lavished on them or which deserve a mention for historic or other reasons. Externally the Church of the Ascension, Timoleague, Co. Cork (1811), is little different from a hundred other country churches, but inside the ceiling, chancel and walls are covered in a glorious mosaic of leaves, flowers and angels interspersed with lotus blossoms and Islamic shapes, creating a fusion of European and Oriental art. This decoration is described by Jeremy Williams as 'a hidden masterpiece of the Arts and Crafts movement in Ireland': it was instigated by the local Travers family as a memorial to deceased relatives, and was completed by the Maharaja of Gwalior in memory of a parishioner, Surgeon General Alymer Crofts (1854–1915), who was his close friend while serving in India and who saved his son's life. Lionel Fleming (1905–70), the journalist and BBC war correspondent, is buried in the grounds.

Further west and splendidly situated overlooking a tiny harbour is St Barrahane's, Castletownsend, Co. Cork (1826 — James Pain), described by Archbishop George Otto Simms as 'that beautiful church on the hill'. Edith Somerville and Martin Ross, authors of *The Irish R.M.*, were parishioners and the former played the organ there for 70 years. She also designed the mosaic floor in the chancel and was responsible for commissioning three stained glass windows by Harry Clarke (1889–1931), the outstanding twentieth-century Irish artist in that medium, described by George Russell as 'one of the strangest geniuses of his time'.

Collon Parish Church, Collon, Co. Louth (1811 — Rev D.A. Beaufort), is unusual on two counts. Firstly, the amateur architect was the rector from 1789 to 1821, and, secondly, he chose as his model the Chapel of King's College, Cambridge. The result, as most critics seem to agree, is a building of considerable charm and an early example of the Gothic Revival in Ireland, with its very large fourteen-light perpendicular east window, tall slender columns and delicate fan-vaulting. The pews face inwards towards the central aisle, and the abstract stained glass was designed by the Reverend Beaufort's daughter, Louisa. A relation, Admiral Francis Beaufort (1774–1857), was the inventor of the Beaufort scale used to measure wind speed. In the churchyard is a memorial to Lieutenant James S. Emerson V.C., killed in the Great War.

St Luke's, Mullaghglass, Co. Armagh (1833 — attributed to William Farrell), which lies in the countryside north-west of Newry, is a neat, orderly and charming building virtually unchanged since it was built. Like Collon it does not have a tower or spire, but there are slim elegant pinnacles at the end of each buttress, five lancet windows in the south and north walls, and pretty circular windows at either side of the west end. There is also an overthrow (or iron arch) with lamp at the entrance to the church grounds.

St Mark's, Armagh (1811 — Francis Johnston), is approached from the Mall by a long and delightful avenue lined by rows of lime trees. This is one of the best churches of the period, with a dignified three-storey tower, over the door of which is the primate's coat of arms. The tower is flanked by elegant buttresses and windows, above which is a castellated roof with tall decorative pinnacles. The interior is equally handsome. Sir Charles Brett describes it as 'an uncommonly attractive church'.

*65. St Mark's Church,
the Mall, Armagh
(1811).*

*66. St Moling's
Church, Borris,
Co. Carlow
(1820).*

St Moling's, Borris, Co. Carlow, is the private chapel of Borris House (1820 — Sir Richard Morrison), to which it was once connected by a gallery, since demolished. It is a delightful little building with a Tudor-style exterior. Borris House was the home of the remarkable Arthur MacMorrough Kavanagh, who was born without arms or legs but led an adventurous and active life in addition to becoming a member of Parliament.

St Cronan's Church, Roscrea, Co. Tipperary (1812), was built to replace the twelfth-century Hiberno-Romanesque church of the same name, the elegant west front of which still stands nearby. It is a fine, spacious, galleried church, with both pulpit and prayer desk designed by Richard Orpen (1863–1938) in memory of the 26 parishioners who lost their lives in the Great War. Remarkably, all ten children of one parishioner, John Nixon, saw active service in that war.

The Church of St Munis, Forgney, Co. Longford (1810), is notable for its connection with the poet Oliver Goldsmith (1728–74), whose father was curate of the previous church on the same site. The Goldsmith Memorial Window in the south wall was installed by admirers in 1897. The church is also noteworthy for the bow-fronted projections of the rooms on either side of the tower at the west end.

The celebrated English architect John Nash (1752–1835) designed St Paul's, Cahir, Co. Tipperary (1817), and incorporated a private entrance and gallery for his patron, the earl of Glengal.

67. St Paul's Church, Cahir, Co. Tipperary (1820).

68. St Mary's Church, Doneraile, Co. Cork (1815).

He also designed the attractive needle spire of St John's Church, Caledon, Co. Tyrone (1768), in 1808.

St Bigseach's, Kilbixy, near Ballynacarrigy, Co. Westmeath (1810), stands on the site of what was once a thriving Norman borough of which nothing remains. It is a very pretty church with a richly ornamented tower and hall but, sadly, part of the roof has collapsed and only a small area remains in use as the parish church. A feature of the grounds is the enormous chestnut tree, while the mausoleum of the Malone family is a reminder of past glories.

Churches with battlemented parapets are not very common, but a good example is the Church of St Philip and St James, Cross Avenue, Booterstown, Co. Dublin (1824 — John Bowden). It is in the Early English style with a fine three-storey crenellated tower and spire, both built of granite. The former is supported by four lofty buttresses capped by gablets, each of which is decorated by four carved stone heads, as are the twelve buttresses supporting the nave. The chancel is the outstanding internal feature and contains a lovely marble panelled reredos erected as a Great War memorial. Among the 40 men commemorated is Lieutenant F.H. Norway, a brother of the novelist Neville Shute (1899–1960). Both were parishioners when their family lived in Ireland.

St Patrick's, Leckpatrick, Artigarvan, Co. Tyrone (1816), is a plain but inviting church with a bellcote, cream-coloured walls and four large round-headed clear glass windows on the south side and a similar but larger window with Gothic glazing bars at the east end. The bright interior is much as it was when built, with high box pews painted grey and a two-decker pulpit in the centre of the south wall, a very rare survival in a nineteenth-century church. Amongst the memorials from a previous church is one dated 1673 to Isabella Sinclair, a rector's wife.

St Mary's, Doneraile, Co. Cork (1815), is built on the site of a 1633 church, and part of the tower probably dates from that time. This church was rebuilt in 1726 by Arthur Viscount Doneraile, a descendant of whom, Colonel St Leger, founded the famous horse race of the same name in 1776. The horse-racing term 'steeplechase' is said to have originated in 1752 when one of the first races over obstacles was run from the steeple of St John's, Buttevant, Co. Cork (1826 — J. and G.R. Pain), to the steeple at Doneraile, the spire of which was destroyed in a storm in 1825 and never replaced. The present church is a charming building both externally and internally and one of the few country churches to have a peal of six bells, installed in 1890. A bell from the 1633 church is on display in the porch. The side windows are set in unusual trefoil-headed rebates, as is the east window, flanked by

69. St Patrick's Church, Monaghan, Co. Monaghan (c. 1836).

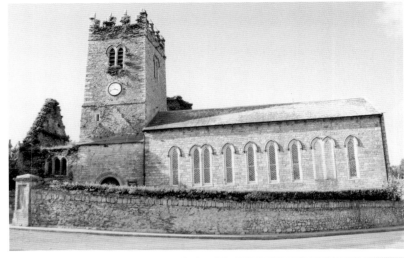

70. St Mary's Church, Inistioge, Co. Kilkenny (1825 — tower twelfth-century).

71. St Catherine's Church, Killoe, Co. Longford (c. 1824).

72. St Mary's, Kilwatermoy, Co. Waterford.

*73. All Saints'
Church,
Castleconnell,
Co. Limerick
(1802).*

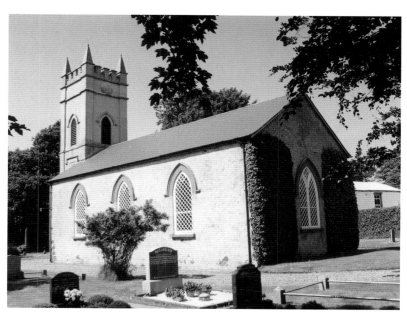

*74. Cloncha
Parish Church,
Malin, Co.
Donegal (1827).*

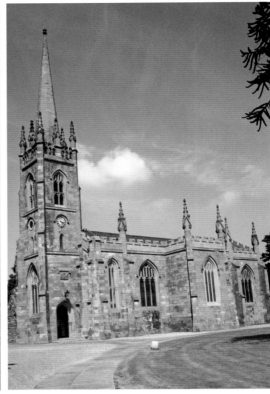

75. (left) One of the more than 100 stone carved heads on the exterior of the old Chapel Royal, Dublin Castle (1814).

76. (right) St Mark's Church, Newtownards, Co. Down (1817).

blank niches. The wooden colonnades in the interior repeat the trefoil theme and the overall effect is bright and cheerful.

Sandford Parish Church, Ranelagh, Co. Dublin (1826), was greatly enhanced in 1860 by an Italianate façade designed by Lanyon, Lynn and Lanyon, while side aisles and a chancel apse were added in 1880. Two fine stained glass windows by Harry Clarke were installed in 1921. The church with its neighbouring small cottage is a most pleasing sight and reminds the viewer of warmer climes.

Because of its association with W.B. Yeats (1865–1939), who is buried in the graveyard and whose grandfather was rector for many years, no other parish church in Ireland has more visitors than St Columba's, Drumcliffe, Co. Sligo (1809). The poet's grave and tombstone with its famous epitaph, written by himself, is a major tourist attraction.

'Cast a cold eye
on life, on death.
Horseman, pass by!'

He was originally buried in the south of France, where he died in 1939, and because of the Second World War it was 1948 before his remains were brought back to Ireland and he was reinterred 'under bare Ben Bulben's head' in Drumcliffe churchyard.

Some 'First Fruits' churches were quite large, and this was especially the case in garrison towns such as Cavan, Fermoy, Monaghan and Templemore, where church attendance was compulsory for the military and where an entire battalion (600–800 men) might parade on a Sunday. St Patrick's, Monaghan, Co. Monaghan (1836 — William Farrell), with its galleries can accommodate a congregation of 1200, while Cavan Parish Church, Cavan, Co. Cavan (1820 — John Bowden), also galleried, has a similar capacity. Both churches contain fine memorials — particularly in Monaghan, where romantic monuments commemorate local heroes who died in distant parts of the British Empire.

St Brendan's, Birr, Co. Offaly (1810 — John Johnston), and St Mary's, Newry, Co. Down (1819 — Patrick O'Farrel), are also large galleried churches with fine interiors. The former is splendidly situated at the end of the Mall opposite Birr Castle and contains magnificent memorials to various earls of Rosse, while the latter is noteworthy for its impressive tower, 60ft spire and splendid east window.

St Columba's, Glencolumcille (1827), in a remote area of County Donegal stands in splendid isolation not far from that village and is an outpost of the Church of Ireland. Another is St Thomas's, Dugort, Achill, Co. Mayo, built between 1833 and 1838 by the Rev. Edward Nangle, founder of the controversial Achill Mission which strove to convert the native Catholic population to Protestantism over a period of nearly 100 years. He also built a church on the small island of Inishbiggle which lies to the east and is now used jointly by islanders of both persuasions. This church and St Thomas's Church on Rathlin Island off the County Antrim coast are the most isolated in the whole of Ireland. At the other end of the country St Paul's, Balloughton, Co. Wexford (1822), is a most surprising sight with its Tudor corner turret running the full height of its tower, as is Kilfane, Co. Kilkenny (1832), with its very odd belfry. St Mary's, Inistioge (1825), in the same county was built incorporating a twelfth-century tower and is a pleasing sight in this riverside village. St John's, Ballinalea, Co. Longford (1830 — John Hargrave), is one of the more charming midland churches, as is St Catherine's, Killoe (1824), in the same county. Other attractive churches include All Saints', Castleconnell, Co. Limerick (1802), St

Mary's, Caheragh, Co. Cork (1829), Holy Trinity, Rathclaren, Co. Cork (1835), St Canice's, Eglinton, Co. Londonderry (1821 — John Bowden), Castleterra Parish Church, Ballyhaise, Co. Cavan (1820), St Davnett's, Ballinode, Co. Monaghan (1830), with its memorial clock-tower, Lorum Church, near Fenagh, Co. Carlow (1806 — probably Fredrick Darley), a distinctive seven-bay, closely buttressed church with steeple erected by Joseph Welland, and Cloncha Parish Church, Malin, Co. Donegal (1827), the most northerly church on the Irish mainland.

Finally, there are two churches which have little in common with their contemporaries. The Chapel Royal, Dublin Castle (1807), is one of the major works of Francis Johnston and is an outstanding building in the Gothic style, rich in every detail with superb plasterwork, woodwork, sculpture and glass. It was the private chapel of the viceroy until 1922 but in 1934 was reconsecrated as the Roman Catholic Church of the Most Holy Trinity.

St Mark's, Newtownards, Co. Down (1817), although not so grand, is similar in certain respects to the Dublin church, mainly in terms of the outside carving, pinnacles and battlemented roof which suggests that it may also have been designed by Johnston. Externally this is a most attractive church which some depict as 'Strawberry Hill Gothic'. However, D.S. Richardson states that 'the exterior is a most exceptional piece of Perpendicular Gothic design; probably the best of its date in the British Isles'. The Londonderry family of Mount Stewart helped with the initial cost and their coat of arms is over the west door.

These two churches, together with those at Hillsborough and Collon, anticipate the Gothic Revival which was to transform church architecture during the remainder of the nineteenth century.

7. THE CHURCHES OF JOHN SEMPLE

The architect John Semple, described by Peter Costello as 'the Lord of creation at the Board of First Fruits', built all of his churches between 1824 and 1831, but his style is so individual that he deserves a chapter to himself. Maurice Craig, a great admirer, praises him for his originality both in the use of barrel-vaulting and in his rejection of all conventional mouldings, and describes his architecture as being 'like Cubist painting, everything being reduced to the severest geometry: buttresses, pinnacles, mouldings — everything in a contrast of planes'. His family were well-known Dublin building contractors with an address at 13 College Green, and his father, also John Semple, built the Round Room of the Mansion House in Dawson Street, while his great-grand-uncle was George Semple who raised the stone spire on St Patrick's Cathedral in 1749. Despite this background we know very little about him as a person, but it is believed that he was born in 1801 and died in 1873. We do know that he was Dublin city architect from 1829 to 1842.

His most remarkable church is St Mary's Chapel of Ease, St Mary's Place, off Dorset Street, Dublin (1830), popularly known as the 'Black Church' because the Dublin calp of which it is built turns black in wet weather. From the outside it is a typical Semple church with closely spaced buttresses, a delicate steeple, fine pinnacles, lancet windows and deep-set west door, but, inside, walls and ceiling are replaced by a parabolic or curved vault, following the practice of ancient Irish churches with their barrel-vaulted roofs. The high and narrow windows lean inwards, and overall the effect is most impressive and unlike any other church in Ireland. It is no longer in use for worship, being occupied by a financial company which has retained its architectural qualities largely intact. There is an extant photograph from 1840 taken by an associate of the pioneer photographer Fox Talbot which shows the exterior virtually unchanged. It used to be said locally that if you walked

To the Glory of GOD
In memory of
The Rt Honble Mr Justice Murphy
of Glencairn.
Died Sept: 5th 1901.

77. *(left)*
Kilternan Parish
Church,
Kilternan, Co.
Dublin (1826).

77a. *(right)*
Stained glass
memorial window
at Kilternan
Parish Church.

twice around the Black Church you would meet the devil.

Holy Trinity Church, Rathmines, Dublin (1828), also had a parabolic roof and, like the Black Church, is built on an island site, making it a well-known local landmark. However, a new roof was installed in 1886 when the building was substantially enlarged to cater for a growing congregation. There was a further major restoration in 1990, when the seating area was reduced and the west end altered to create a parish hall, but, externally at least, it remains essentially a Semple church with all the usual features, including the delightfully slender tower and spire. The war memorial records the names of 60 parishioners killed in the Great War, and there is fine stained glass by Michael Healy and Alfred E. Child in the north transept.

One of his most appealing churches is Kilternan Parish Church, Kilternan, Co. Dublin (1826), described by the topographer Samuel Lewis shortly after its consecration as 'a handsome edifice in the late English Gothic style'. It is built entirely of granite obtained from the local quarries, which must have pleased the then archbishop, William Magee, who is said to have considered it

78. West door of Kilternan Parish Church, Co. Dublin.

essential that all Protestant churches be able to withstand a siege. Notwithstanding its sturdiness, it is a lovely little building with the usual buttresses surmounted by gablets, a tall, narrow, receding west door and a slender pinnacled tower with a delicate spire. A nineteenth-century painting by George Petrie shows the church exactly as it is today. The interior is bright and cheerful with commemorative stained glass by Sir Ninian Comper and A.K. Nicholson.

A few miles away, in the foothills of the Dublin mountains, is Whitechurch, near Rathfarnham, Co. Dublin (1826), which is similar to Kilternan and equally attractive. It is also granite-built with, perhaps, the most elegant spire of any of Semple's churches and a lovely sight when seen from afar. Inside, five massive timber arches (plastered over to appear as stone) span the nave, a common feature in many of his churches. In 1997 a stained glass window was installed by the businessman and kidnap victim Don Tidey and his family to give thanks for the eighteen years during which they were members of the congregation.

79. Whitechurch, near Rathfarnham, Co. Dublin (1826).

St Maelruain's, Tallaght, Co. Dublin (1829), is situated on the site of an eighth-century monastery and provides an oasis of calm in an otherwise hectic suburb. This church has no tower and, instead, there are massive buttresses at the four corners, each capped by four pinnacles, with a central pinnacle more like a small spire. Pinnacles also top each of the other buttresses. Inside are the characteristic arches, while the walls have been stripped to bare stone to give a bright, dignified interior. The tower of an ancient church survives alongside and continues in use as a belfry.

St Mary's, Donnybrook, Dublin (1825), is one of his bigger churches, with more buttresses than usual and numerous pinnacles. An early nineteenth-century painting by George Petrie shows it on an open site with an elegant spire, but the latter was removed following storm damage in 1839. Inside, the walls are stripped to bare stone and there is fine stained glass and the font in which W.B. Yeats was baptised in 1865. Large pointed arches in yellow brick lead to the chancel and transepts, while arches also span the crossing and the nave. As at Rathmines, the west end of the nave has been blocked off to create a parochial hall.

There are five of his churches outside County Dublin still in use. The largest and finest is Abbeyleix Parish Church, Abbeyleix, Co. Laois (1830), which was also built with a parabolic vault. However, this ceiling was replaced and today only the west end of the church with its lovely tower and spire can be attributed to Semple. In the adjoining county is Killeshin, Co. Carlow (1826), which also has an attractive tower and steeple but no buttresses. The only jarring feature here is the badly placed door in the south wall, which must be a later addition. St Patrick's, Newbridge, Co. Kildare (1824), lacks a spire but has a fine tower and, typically, there are four sturdy arches spanning the nave to match the exterior buttresses. Cloneyhurke, Co. Offaly (1831), is similar with a pleasing exterior, but the finish is not up to his usual standard. Rathangan, Co. Kildare (1831), is also without a spire and, except for the west end, has few of the usual Semple characteristics. The north wall is windowless.

Semple built three other country churches at about the same time. Ballykeen (or Killeighy), Clonygowan, Co. Offaly, has been demolished, and Thomastown, Co. Kildare, suffered the same fate. The sole survivor is Feighcullen, east of Rathangan, Co. Kildare, which, though still standing, is in very poor condition. It is very true to type with all the expected features, including a slender spire and three massive internal arches. Although a sorry and

80. (above)
Abbeyleix Parish
Church,
Abbeyleix, Co.
Laois (1830).

81. (above right)
Killeshin Church,
near Carlow, Co.
Carlow (1826).

82. (right)
Cloneyhurke
Church, Co.
Offaly (1831).

depressing sight now, it must have been a very attractive church in its heyday. It is currently a protected building and planning permission is being sought to repair the roof and guttering, but to what end is not certain. Its future must be considered precarious.

His last and most controversial church is Monkstown Parish Church, Monkstown, Co. Dublin, which held its first service on Christmas Day 1831. It immediately attracted a great deal of criticism and was variously described as 'a nondescript edifice which disfigures its site' and 'a grotesque piece of architecture adorned with curious little pinnacles, the rounded curves of which recall the familiar pawn at chess'. Others pronounced it 'a glorious Portuguese extravaganza' and 'castellated Gothic with Moorish elements'. With palm trees under its battlements it is more like an Arabian castle than a church, but today, on its conspicuous site in the heart of busy Monkstown, it seems very much at ease with its surroundings. Internally, there are two large transepts with galleries entered through the tall narrow doorways so typical of Semple. There is also a gallery at the west end and a splendid chancel, all framed by the familiar massive arches on equally

83. Part of the southern aspect of Monkstown Parish Church, Co. Dublin (1831).

massive corbels. The walls are of sandstone blocks in a variety of pastel shades, while the ceiling is a series of vaults with elegant fan-vaulting at each corner. The fittings are very fine and there is a good collection of memorials. This is a lovely church and Semple's masterpiece. Sir John Betjeman (1906–84), the English Poet Laureate, described it as 'bold, modern, vast and original', and was so fond of it that he became the first patron of the 'Friends of Monkstown' inaugurated in 1974 to preserve the church and its ministry.

All of these churches were built in a period of less than ten years and mostly while John Semple was in his twenties. Brian de Breffny and George Mott rate him as 'the most interesting architect in Ireland in the first half of the nineteenth century but an isolated figure in his time'. An enigmatic character to the end, his death is said to have been reported in the *Building News* some years before his actual demise.

8. TEAMPALL NA MBOCHT

There is one mid-nineteenth-century church whose origins are different to all others and whose story is worth telling. This is Teampall na mBocht (the Church of the Poor) at Toormore, not far from Mizen Head in west County Cork.

This part of the country was wild and remote in 1846 when the Great Famine struck, causing terrible local suffering and huge loss of life. The rector at nearby Goleen (now deconsecrated) was the Rev. William Allen Fisher, who soon found himself isolated when the rectors of Schull and Skibbereen, the only clergy near at hand, died of famine fever. At the same time, the local parish priest, who was not on good terms with his flock, fled the community and left his parishioners to fend for themselves. There was no resident landlord and Fisher had to provide what relief he could. With money sent from England and from his own resources he set up soup kitchens, in addition to visiting the poor in their cabins; this led to his contracting famine fever, from which he nearly died. As the people were still without a priest and had no one to go to for

84. Teampall na mBocht, Toormore, Co. Cork (1847).

spiritual solace, Fisher, a fluent Irish-speaker and a man with Tractarian and High Church sympathies, let it be known that he would be prepared to hear confessions from anyone who cared to approach him. A few did, and then so many that his entire day was occupied with them. This was followed by a mass embrace of the Church of Ireland, so that it became necessary to build a chapel of ease. This work was undertaken by the new converts in the winter of 1847 and completed the following year. These events caused great concern in the Roman Catholic Church, and Father John Murphy, the militant son of a wealthy Cork merchant, was sent to bring the apostates back to the papal fold. Over the years the majority returned to their traditional faith, but it is believed that as many as 600 remained Protestant for the rest of their lives. Whatever the outcome, the Reverend Foster retained the people's love and respect until he died, aged 72, having again contracted fever when helping a stricken family during the famine of 1880. The simple church at Toormore is a lasting and fitting memorial to this good and faithful pastor.

9. THE NINETEENTH-CENTURY GOTHIC REVIVAL

The Victorian era lasted from 1837 to 1901 and was an age of great change, not least in church architecture where the Classical style became outmoded and there was a revival of interest in the Gothic of the Middle Ages. Of the 214 churches built in England by state grants early in Queen Victoria's reign over 170 were in the Gothic style.

This was largely due to the influence of Augustus Welby Northmore Pugin (1812–52). Born an Anglican, he converted to the Roman Catholic church in 1835 and was a man of trenchant and passionate views who hated Classical architecture, which he associated with paganism. He is said to have told a senior prelate that 'the only thing worse than Classicism is Socialism', and he denigrated architectural pattern-books as being 'as bad as the scriptures in the hands of Protestants'. He declared that the only true church architecture could be Gothic. For him it was not simply a style but a principle, a moral crusade, and the only mode of building for a Christian nation.

The Church of Ireland was won over, and many of the old auditory and simple 'First Fruits' churches were modified as a result. Long chancels with steps from the nave were added and the plain Georgian glass replaced by stained glass. Box pews were removed and three-decker pulpits were superseded by a separate pulpit and lectern. The font was moved to the west end and the choir to the chancel. Some churches were reorientated, as at Christ Church, Taney, Co. Dublin (1818), where the old building on a north–south axis was transformed by Joseph Welland in 1862 when he added a chancel to the east and a new nave to the west, leaving the body of the original church as the transepts. The same thing happened in 1877 at St Mark's, Ligoniel Road, Belfast (1854), and at Tullow Church, Carrickmines, Co. Dublin (1864 — Welland and Gillespie).

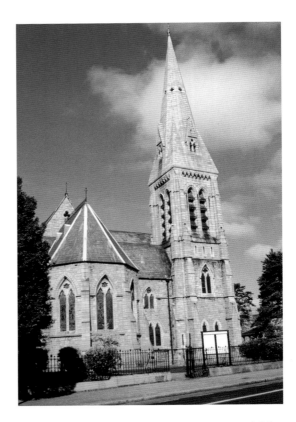

*85. Christ Church,
Leeson Park, Dublin
(1862).*

Others were completely transformed, as at St Patrick's, Coleraine, Co. Londonderry (1614). The seventeenth-century building had been added to repeatedly in the early nineteenth century but was virtually rebuilt by Sir Thomas Drew in 1883. The present church is large and decorative with many interesting memorials, but the most striking feature is the massive western tower complete with gargoyles and fine carvings by a local craftsman, Charles Magowan. Lying in the heart of Coleraine, it dominates the shopping centre and, in Simon Walker's words, 'stands as a seemly and well-conceived example of Victorian church architecture'.

Owing to increases in population large new Gothic Revival churches (as they came to be known) were built in the cities and these incorporated all of the features described above, with the addition of imposing towers and spires, high roofs and gables. Dublin led the way with St Andrew's Church, St Andrew's Street (1862 — W.H. Lynn), and Christ Church, Leeson Park (1862 — Rawson Carroll). Both could seat congregations of over 1000 but the former was deconsecrated in 1995 and is now the Dublin

Tourism Centre. At one time Christ Church had a pauper's gallery close to the chancel where the undesirables of the parish could be heard but not seen as they were hidden from the congregation by heavy curtains.

St Bartholomew's Church (1864 — T.H. Wyatt), Clyde Road, Dublin, has a commanding exterior and beautiful interior, the inspiration for which is said to be the Sicilian cathedral of Monreale. The frescoes and paintings designed by Sir Thomas Deane in the sanctuary are Byzantine in style and wonderfully colourful and exotic in an Irish church. There is also a fine decorated organ of 1884 and stained glass by Catherine O'Brien and Michael O'Connor. The choir is one of the few in Ireland with only men and boys and has been a feature of the church for over 100 years.

As Dublin expanded in the middle of the nineteenth century wealthy suburbs were created with large churches such as St John the Baptist, Clontarf (1866 — Joseph Welland), St Mary's, Howth (1866 — J.E. Rogers), St Paul's, Glenageary (1868 — Alfred Jones), Zion Church, Rathgar (1861 — Joseph Welland), All Saints' Church, Raheny (1889 — George C. Ashlin), and St Jude's, Inchicore. The latter is deconsecrated with its nave dismantled and moved to Sallins, Co. Kildare, where it houses the steam museum. The abandoned tower and spire still stand and a new owner is being sought.

Of all these suburban churches All Saints', Raheny, is outstanding and one of the most beautiful in the country. It was

86. St Bartholomew's Church, Ballsbridge, Dublin (1864).

87. The font at All Saints' Church, Raheny, Co. Dublin (1889).

erected at the personal expense of Lord Ardilaun and contains a mortuary chapel where he and Lady Ardilaun are interred. Lord Ardilaun, a member of the Guinness family, is commemorated by his statue in St Stephen's Green, the park he gifted to the citizens of Dublin. Built to the highest standards, the church contains finely carved pews and pulpit, lovely stained glass and interior walls of Caen stone. There is a beautiful font on marble columns with a suspended brass cover, while the original oil lamps are still in place. The external craftsmanship is equally fine, with a spire modelled on Salisbury Cathedral. Mrs Annabella Jane Hayes, wife of the first rector, was founder of the Mother's Union in Ireland in 1887.

In Belfast, where the population increased by 300,000 between 1851 and 1911, there was a church-building boom, much of it in the Gothic Revival style. It was also a period of outstanding church architects, including Sir Charles Lanyon (1813–89), W.J. Barre (1830–67), Sir Thomas Drew (1838–1910) and Joseph Welland (1798–1860). Welland built more than 100 churches and was sole architect to the Ecclesiastical Commissioners (which replaced the Board of First Fruits in 1833) from 1838 until his death.

One of the earliest and most impressive is St Thomas's, Eglantine Avenue (1845 — Sir John Lanyon), built in the Early French Gothic style with a polychromatic exterior popular at this period and a fine arcaded tower and spire with red marble colonettes. The large and striking interior has six red-bricked arches along both aisles and is fitted with good-quality furnishings, including a splendid reredos.

St Mary's, Crumlin Road (1865–8 — William Slater), is another large impressive church with a massive arcaded tower surmounted by a small broach spire with walls of white stone banded in red. This theme is repeated internally, with all of the pointed arches in chancel, sanctuary, aisles and windows in alternative red and white stone which creates an exotic effect. When first built there were hopes that it would become Belfast's first cathedral but these were never realised. It was badly damaged in 1941 during the heavy German air raids. Today, St Mary's lies in an area blighted by the civil disturbances of the late twentieth century and is badly in need of renewal and redevelopment. Nearly 300 men of the parish were killed in the Great War.

St Mark's Church, Dundela, Holywood Road (1876–91 — William Butterfield), is one of the finest built during the reign of Queen Victoria. Its tall four-storey tower with scaled roof dominates the surrounding suburbs and is of red sandstone in line with the rest of the exterior. The tall interior has a hammerbeam roof, while the arches in the nave are supported by alternate round and octagonal pillars. The altar and beautiful reredos stand taller than the pulpit, putting the emphasis on the altar in line with the architect's Tractarian views. The large baptistry is beneath the west tower and a single slender colonette supports its traceried arch. The pews have exceptionally low backs as it was thought (though not proven) that this would force worshippers to their knees during prayers. In the south wall is a stained glass window by Michael Healy erected by the writer C.S. Lewis (1898–1963) and his brother Warnie in memory of their mother and father. The Rev. Thomas Hamilton, first rector of St Mark's, was their grandfather. William Butterfield (1814–1900), an Englishman, is one of the great Gothic Revival architects but his only other Irish church is St Columba's College Chapel, near Rathfarnham, Co. Dublin (1880), a dignified building with a delicately carved alabaster pulpit, a carved lectern of Caen stone and a memorial on the north wall to the five masters and 67 past pupils (all officers) who died in the Great War.

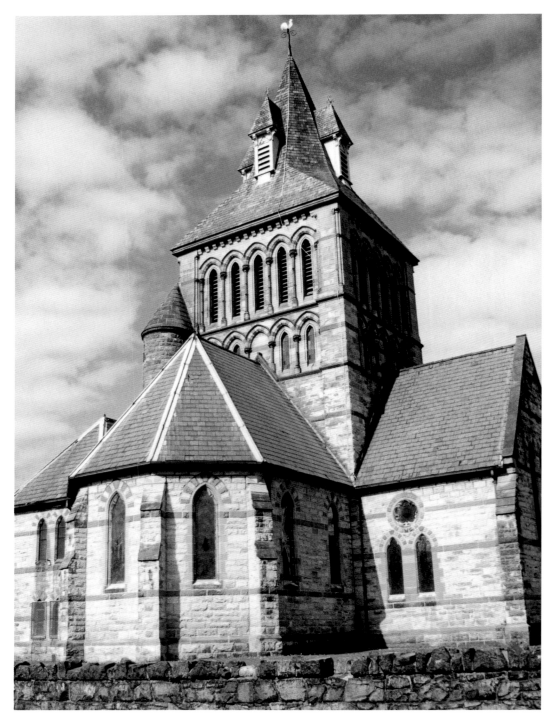

88. St Mary's Church, Crumlin Road, Belfast (1868).

89. (above) St Mark's Church, Dundela, Co. Down (1878).

90. (left) Altar and reredos of St Mark's Church, Dundela, Co. Down.

Other notable Belfast churches include Willowfield, Woodstock Road (Sir John Lanyon — 1871/2), St Jude's, Ormeau Road (Sir Thomas Drew — 1871–3), and the Church of St John the Evangelist, Malone Road (Henry Seaver — 1893–1905). The latter includes fine stained glass by Evie Hone (1894–1955), Wilhelmina Geddes (1888–1955) and Catherine O'Brien (1881–1963), who with Michael Healy (1873–1941) and Alfred E. Child (1875–1939) were prominent artists in An Tur Gloine (the Tower of Glass), the celebrated Dublin stained glass studio founded in 1903 by Sarah Purser (1848–1943). Catherine O'Brien's work can be seen in no fewer than 75 churches and Alfred Child's in 51.

Throughout Ulster there are scores of fine Gothic Revival churches, and Holywood Parish Church, Holywood, Co. Down (1844 — Sir Charles Lanyon), St Columba's, Omagh, Co. Tyrone (1870 — J.E. Rogers), St Donard's, Dundrum, Co. Down (1886 — Sir Thomas Drew), St Luke's, Ballymoyer, Co. Armagh (1865 — W.J. Barre), All Saints', Waterside, Co. Londonderry (1864–7 — Lanyon, Lynn and Lanyon), Holy Trinity, Carrigart, Co. Donegal (1895 — Sir Thomas Drew), Clanabogan Parish Church, near Omagh, Co. Tyrone (1861 — Welland and Gillespie), St Margaret's, Clabby, Co. Fermanagh (1864–7 — Welland and Gillespie), St

91. (right) Stained glass window of St Brigid at St John's Church, Malone Road, Belfast. (Evie Hone.)

92. (below) Detail from the stained glass east window of St Mary's Church, Clonmel, Co. Tipperary. (Catherine O'Brien.)

Swithin's, Magherafelt, Co. Londonderry (1856 — Joseph Welland), St Bride's, Doagh, Co. Antrim (1868 — Welland and Gillespie), and St Anne's, Dungannon, Co. Tyrone (1865 — W.J. Barre), are but a small selection. The last named is most impressive and dominates Dungannon with its huge clock-tower, spire and west gable. The interior, with its fine pulpit and font, is correspondingly spacious with two very large transepts, high arches, an enormous rose window and unusually tall windows in the nave. It is believed to be an adaptation of Barre's competition entry for St Fin Barre's Cathedral in Cork and is considered his finest work. Tragically, he died only a few years after its completion at the age of 37.

The Church of Christ the Redeemer, Lurgan, Co. Armagh (1867 — Welland and Gillespie), with its galleries on three sides has a seating capacity of 2000, making it the largest parish church in Ireland. With its sizeable clock-tower and spire it is an imposing building in the heart of the town. The font is dated 1684 and a 1696 silver chalice is still in use.

There are two lovely churches by Sir Thomas Drew in County Fermanagh. St Patrick's, Castle Archdale (1908), on the northern shore of Lower Lough Erne, with gryphons on its tower, has a charming interior with walls of pale sandstone, an oak wagon roof and a splendid carved oak pulpit. It is described by Alistair Rowan as 'an extremely attractive church with workmanship of great quality: a perfect example of an Arts and Crafts taste'.

Considered by Jeremy Williams 'a minor masterpiece', Devenish Parish Church, Monea (1890), on the south side of the lake has an equally appealing interior not unlike St Patrick's. A most interesting and rare feature is the 1445 two-light window brought from Devenish Abbey, as was the black stone font.

Holy Trinity Church, Crom, Co. Fermanagh (1842), is picturesquely sited on the Derryvore Peninsula and is surrounded on three sides by the waters of Upper Lough Erne. It has a four-bay nave to which a chancel and vault were added in 1869. Those buried in the vault include Selina, countess of Erne, in whose memory a belfry tower with abutting octagonal stair turret was added in 1888. There is a fine east window, unusually high pews in the aisle and a large box pew at the west end. In the late nineteenth and early twentieth centuries the local gentry sailed to Holy Trinity for service each Sunday in their private steamers and landed at the little pier below the church. During the same period the lake was a great yachting centre where the local wealthy families designed

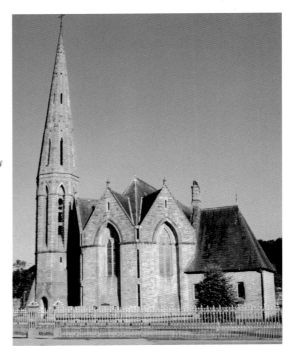

93. Church of the Holy Trinity, Westport, Co. Mayo (1872).

and built their own boats. Royalty and the viceroy were frequent visitors to the Lough Erne Yacht Club up to 1914 but the losses suffered in the Great War and ensuing events in Ireland brought this brilliant era to an abrupt end.

The outstanding church of the period in Connacht is Holy Trinity, Westport, Co. Mayo (1868 — T.N. Deane), which replaced the church of 1797 built in the grounds of Westport House, where the ruins can still be seen. The interior houses murals and mosaics by Italian craftsmen, the most striking of which is the depiction of Leonardo da Vinci's 'The Last Supper' over the west door. Other outstanding features include the stained glass windows, the sanctuary of Carrara marble and the lovely carved alabaster pulpit. The rector from 1892 to 1913 was Canon James Hannay, who achieved literary fame under the *nom de plume* George A. Bermingham.

Further south in County Galway is St John the Baptist's, Eyrecourt (1867 — William Martin), which has a steeply pitched roof and an impressive south porch. The internal walls are of red brick except for relieving bands in black and white, and there is a west gallery and beautiful windows in the nave. Angels form the corbels on each side of the chancel arch, under which is a fine sandstone pulpit and lectern. Suspended from the high ceiling are four original circular chandeliers, each containing twelve candles, and there is a large collection of interesting memorials to parishioners who served and died in remote parts of the British Empire and South America.

St Peter's, Bandon, Co. Cork (1849 — Joseph Welland), is one of the finest Victorian churches in Munster and replaced a previous one at Ballymodan built in 1614. It is in the Decorated Gothic style, with a bell-tower 110ft high and an interior which is spacious, airy and imposing. It has a lovely chancel and sanctuary, fine stained glass and splendid memorials, including one to the last earl of Bandon, Percy R.G. Bernard (1904–79), who was Air Chief Marshal of the Royal Air Force. The pulpit by J.F. Fuller is of Caen stone, marble and alabaster and very beautiful, as is the brass eagle lectern. The church silver dates back to 1630 and is of high quality. A pulpit similar to the one at St Peter's was gifted by the Church of Ireland to St George's Cathedral, Jerusalem, in 1898.

Further west in County Kerry is the fine parish church of St

94. South porch of the church of St John the Baptist, Eyrecourt, Co. Galway (1867).

*95. Pulpit at St Peter's
Church, Bandon, Co.
Cork (photo: Bob
Wright).*

© 1999 Bob Wright

Mary's, Killarney (1870 — William Atkins), situated in the heart of
that tourist mecca. It was destroyed by fire in 1888 but rebuilt by
J.F. Fuller. It has an impressive four-storey buttressed tower
surmounted by a small spire, and is cruciform in design with arches
dividing the nave from the transepts and chancel. The latter has
three windows with good stained glass, one panel depicting the
infant Jesus with a beard. A special feature is the hand-
embroidered peacock on the altar frontal which dates from 1959.
Also by William Atkins and in a beautiful waterside setting on the
estuary of the River Lee is Gurranekennefeake Church, East Ferry,
Co. Cork (*c.* 1870). It has a fine arcaded tower and a spire with
lucarnes and is built of red sandstone with white bands. Jeremy
Williams aptly describes it as 'being like a cathedral from afar but
a tiny wayside chapel close up'. In this quiet part of County Cork
it is a very pleasant surprise.

St Columba's, Ennis, Co. Clare (1871 — W.H. Lynn), is an
uncommonly large church for this part of Ireland. It has a good
saddle-roofed tower and internally its finest feature is the chancel
and sanctuary, which incorporates a wide intricate reredos

depicting the Virgin Mary and a variety of saints and apostles, all sculpted by James Leech and set in a mosaic framework by Catherine O'Brien. The stained glass windows in the porch are by the same artist in memory of her sisters.

South Leinster is home to some excellent Gothic Revival churches, with St Saviour's, Arklow, Co. Wicklow (1899 — Sir Arthur Blomfield), outstanding. Built at the sole expense of the fifth earl of Carysfort, it is in the Early English style with a massive tower and spire reaching to a height of 154ft. The vaulted oak ceiling of the nave is supported by green marble columns, while the outstanding internal feature is the soaring west arch beneath which is sited the font with its carved oak canopy. Every other item is of high quality, with the pulpit, organ case and altar carved out of American walnut. There are richly carved bosses in the roof and the stained glass is by Clayton and Bell.

Christ Church, Bray, Co. Wicklow (1860–70 — William Slater), is one of the largest parish churches. Built of granite with a formidable tower and spire housing a peal of eight bells, it is a tall building with clear clerestory windows and a magnificent five-light east window in memory of the tenth earl of Meath. The outstanding features include the arcaded sanctuary and reredos filled with Venetian glass mosaic and the splendidly carved lectern, prayer desk and bishop's chair made by the local Bray Art Furniture Industry, founded in 1887.

Christ Church, Gorey, Co. Wexford (1859–61 — Joseph Welland), is another big church which not only has a fine square tower and belfry but also a round tower and large gable with a

96. Altar and reredos at the Adelaide Memorial Church, Myshall, Co. Carlow (photo: Muriel Broadberry).

*97. Adelaide Memorial
Church of Christ the
Redeemer, Myshall, Co.
Carlow (1913).*

Catherine-wheel window facing the main street. The special internal feature is the memorial stained glass windows by Harry Clarke, erected in 1922, to the murdered police superintendent Captain Lea-Wilson. There is also glass by the ubiquitous Catherine O'Brien.

Two other notable Gothic churches are Holy Trinity, Castlemacadam, Avoca, Co. Wicklow (1868 — probably W.H. Lynn), with its saddle-roofed tower, and Kilbride, near Enniskerry, Co. Wicklow (1857 — W.J. Barre), which is considered a masterpiece of originality and was designed by the architect when he was only 24.

One of the last churches built before the Great War, and among the most beautiful belonging to the Church of Ireland, is the Adelaide Memorial Church of Christ the Redeemer in the tiny village of Myshall, Co. Carlow (1913 — George Ashlin). It was built at the sole expense of John Duguid Dover of Cornwall, whose daughter Constance had come to Ireland to marry a local landowner but who died tragically in a hunting accident soon afterwards. Following her death her father erected an outdoor Sicilian marble statue of Innocence to her memory, but when this began to deteriorate owing to the weather he decided to build a church where it could be housed and which would be her burial place, and eventually that of his wife Adelaide and himself. The result is a cathedral-like building in the Early English Gothic style with heavily buttressed limestone external walls, high-pitched roofs and gables, lancet windows, a decorative tower, and an elegant spire and weather-vane. The interior, including the roof, is lined with creamy Bath stone which brings a feeling of warmth, and the decoration throughout is of the highest standard. Immediately opposite the entrance is the baptistry, with a lovely marble and alabaster font inlaid with lapis lazuli and mother of pearl. The mosaic floor in the chancel is said to have been copied from St Mark's Cathedral in Venice, while the mosaic reredos depicting the Last Supper is in the style of Leonardo da Vinci. The stained glass is very striking, especially in the nave where the style is Art Nouveau, and the colouring is mainly black and white, matching the mosaic floor. The lectern, pulpit and choir stalls are of oak and finely carved, while the original oil standard lamps are still in use but electrified. There is decoration everywhere with ever-changing designs. The mortuary chapel in the north transept holds the family remains and the statue of Innocence, which is contained within a delicate but intricate wrought-iron and copper screen. It depicts a young girl holding a dove and is placed on a 6ft-high pedestal. Behind the statue Constance is interred in a tomb of polished granite bearing an inscription which, *inter alia*, reads:

> 'Earth holds one gentle soul the less
> and heaven one angel more'.

10. THE NINETEENTH-CENTURY
CELTIC REVIVAL

After Catholic Emancipation in 1829 the position of the Church of Ireland as the state church became less secure, and as the nineteenth century progressed the demand for change became more insistent. There was understandable agitation by Roman Catholics against the paying of tithes (taxes amounting to one tenth of income for the church's upkeep), and in the aftermath of the Great Famine and the 1861 census, which showed that only one person in eight on the island belonged to its flock, the government was forced to take action. Finally, against much opposition, it was disestablished by an Act of 1869 forced through the House of Commons by the Liberal government under W.E. Gladstone.

Disestablishment was a perilous time, but in the spirit of the age both clergy and laity met the danger with vigour and imagination. They agreed how the church was to be governed and made the fullest use of the finances at their disposal. They also looked back to the time when the Celtic church had its own unique and distinctive culture and order, and this was reflected in a revival of the pre-Norman style in architecture. The result was the building of a small number of distinctive and beautiful churches which drew their inspiration from early Irish churches, high crosses, round towers and other ancient artefacts. J.F. Fuller (1835–1924), a Kerryman, was the leading architect of this style, with four churches in counties Kildare and Laois to his credit.

St Patrick's Church, Jordanstown, Co. Antrim (1868 — W.H. Lynn), has been described as the first attempt in modern times to revive the ancient architecture of Ireland. Its inspiration is St Finnian's Church at Clonmacnoise, Co. Offaly, where, atypically, the round tower is attached to the building and this is repeated here. Inside the porch there is a carved stone tympanum of St Patrick as a slave-boy by Rosamund Praegar. The outstanding internal feature is the sanctuary, with its handsome arcade of eight arches on each side of the altar, each filled with mosaics and surmounted by Celtic motifs. Above is the reredos in Derbyshire marble and four good-quality stained glass windows depicting the great Irish saints Patrick, Brigid, Columba and Comgall. The church furnishings are of high quality, and especially attractive are the pair of carved wooden prayer desks supported by angels.

St Michael and All Angels, Clane, Co. Kildare (J.F. Fuller — 1883), was erected at the sole expense of a local landlord, Thomas Cooke-Trench, and is an attractive building of limestone and red sandstone with a lofty tower approached from the road through a lych-gate. The interior is based on Cormac's Chapel at Cashel, Co. Tipperary, and the view of the chancel and sanctuary from the nave is very striking, with a succession of beautifully carved Romanesque arches leading the eye to the altar and the splendid windows behind. Everywhere there is decoration and embellishment, with over 150 stone capitals, corbels and bosses, no two of which are alike. It lives up to its name with archangels over the eastern

98. St Patrick's Church, Jordanstown, Co. Antrim (1868).

99. Church of St Michael and All Angels, Clane, Co. Kildare (1883).

arches, around the western rose window and in the sanctuary. Lord Dunraven in his 'Notes on Irish architecture' wrote that 'Ireland has a national style of architecture capable of exquisite beauty especially adapted to buildings of moderate size', and this is true of Clane and Fuller's other Hiberno-Romanesque-type churches.

The Church of the Ascension, Rathdaire, Ballybrittas, Co. Laois (1883 — J.F. Fuller), was built at the sole expense of an American heiress in memory of her husband. He was the notorious John Adair, who expelled hundreds of tenants from his estate in County Donegal so that he could build the castle and demesne at Glenbeigh. Internally, it is similar to Clane but less decorative. There are fine fittings and nicely carved pews, with a gallery and rose window at the west end. The gallery and the apse at the east end are not features of ancient Irish churches, but otherwise it is entirely in the Hiberno-Romanesque style. The outstanding feature is the west door and façade, which has no equal in a Church of Ireland country church. It is a full-size replica of the west front of the Romanesque church of St Cronan at Roscrea, Co. Tipperary, with additional decorations and carvings from a variety of sources, including the high crosses at Ahenny in the same county. Maurice Craig has described it as 'an extraordinary sight'.

St Patrick's, Carnalway, Co. Kildare, was erected in 1792 and its tower and spire date from that time. Otherwise it was completely rebuilt by J.F. Fuller in 1889, with the addition of a Romanesque porch surmounted by the La Touche coat of arms. Internally it is similar to Clane and Rathdaire, but smaller. Four beautifully

100. *West door of the Church of the Ascension, Rathdaire, Co. Laois (1883).*

101. *Stained glass window of the Holy Family by A.E. Child at Rathmichael Church, Shankill, Co. Dublin.*

102. *Memorial Celtic cross in the grounds of Rathmichael Church, Shankill, Co. Dublin.*

103. *Coolcarrigan Church, Timahoe, Co. Kildare (1885).*

proportioned carved arches mark the intersection of the nave, chancel and transepts, and the windows at the east end are enriched with carvings in Celtic designs and filled with delicately worked stained glass by Sir Ninian Comper (1864–1960), one of the great English church architects of the period, who also designed the lovely reredos. In the south wall there is a marvellous small stained glass window by Harry Clarke in memory of John La Touche, the last member of the famous Huguenot family to live in the district.

Rathmichael, Shankill, Co. Dublin (1862 — Benjamin Woodward), is, by comparison, of simple design and much less decorative. When first built it consisted of nave and chancel only, but towards the end of the nineteenth century a north aisle and south porch were added by T. N. Deane. There is a beautiful font and a pulpit by J.F. Fuller, while the stained glass is of high quality with work by Catherine O'Brien, A.E. Child and Sarah Purser. The exterior walls are of granite with a bellcote at the west end surmounted by a Celtic cross, while below is a lovely wheel window similar to the one at Rahan Church, Co. Offaly. The Celtic cross in the grounds is in memory of a former rector.

Coolcarrigan Church, Timahoe, Co. Kildare (1885 — probably J.F. Fuller), is described by Jeremy Williams as 'the most perfect example of the Celtic Revival' and, like Jordanstown, its design is based on St Finnian's, Clonmacnoise. Small in scale and beautifully proportioned, with a miniature round tower and nearby high cross, it is situated on an ancient motte and surrounded by trees and shrubs. The interior has stained glass by Catherine O'Brien and

104. St Matthew's Church, Shankill Road, Belfast (1872).

105. St Patrick's Church, Ballyclog, Co. Tyrone (1865).

splendid fittings with the wall texts in Celtic script designed by Dr Douglas Hyde. It is maintained at the sole expense of the Wilson-Wright family, who offer it to other denominations as and when the need arises. This is one of the most delightful churches on the island of Ireland, with the added attraction of no collection except on special occasions!

St Matthew's (1872 — Welland and Gillespie) is situated, somewhat incongruously, on the Shankill Road in the heart of Loyalist Belfast. Sir Charles Brett describes it as 'a wholly astonishing building with an originality and a structural daring that make it stand out from the ruck of Victorian churches'. The

106. Ruins of Ballyclog Old Church, Ballyclog, Co. Tyrone (seventeenth century).

107. St Patrick's Church, Saul, Co. Down (1933).

layout is like a shamrock and completely unconventional, with the north, south and east walls forming three apse-like semicircles supported on four ribs springing from slim Corinthian columns. The stem of this trefoil is the organ loft with its rose window. Externally there is a round tower in yellow brick, and the rest of the building is similarly constructed but relieved by red and white brick bands. St Matthew's is unique, but Welland and Gillespie did build another church which bears some resemblance. This is St Patrick's, Ballyclog, Co. Tyrone (1865), with a similar round tower and of polychromatic construction. Alistair Rowan describes it as 'a roguish little building wilfully adapting Irish architectural elements to jazzy ends'. Opposite are the charming ruins of the seventeenth-century Ballyclog Old Church.

St Patrick's, Saul, Co. Down (1933 — Henry Seaver), was erected on land said to have been given to Ireland's patron saint by a local chieftain as the site of his first church in 432. It is small and simple as befits its surroundings, and with its steeply pitched roof and attached round tower it seems likely that St Finnian's was again the inspiration. The interior is plain with a very devotional atmosphere enhanced by the dimly lit chancel, where a solitary small stained glass window by Catherine O'Brien depicts Saint Patrick with his crozier. A visit to this modest church in one of the first places where Christianity was introduced into Ireland is a moving experience.

11. OTHER VICTORIAN AND EDWARDIAN CHURCHES

While Gothic architecture was undoubtedly the fashionable and prevalent style in the Victorian period and the early twentieth century, some churches drew their inspiration from other sources.

The Church of St John the Evangelist (1850 — Benjamin Ferrey), near the sea at Sandymount, Co. Dublin, is a marvellous example of neo-Norman architecture and the only church of its kind in Ireland. It was built by Sydney Herbert at the instigation of his wife, who saw a church in Normandy which she liked and which is replicated here. It is a sturdy building of Caen stone with thick walls, large pillars, deeply recessed doorways, and semicircular arches and windows. The three-storey square tower has a turret attached and a stone roof, while sculptured heads decorate the overhanging eaves and many of the windows. There is also a splendid carved dragon entwined around the vestry chimney. The liturgical tradition is Anglo-Catholic and there are Stations of the

108. The Church of St John the Evangelist, Sandymount, Co. Dublin (1850).

109. The vestry chimney at the Church of St John the Evangelist, Sandymount, Co. Dublin.

Cross, crucifixes and confessionals, making it unique in the Church of Ireland. This was another favourite church of Sir John Betjeman, who worshipped here when he lived in Dublin as British Attaché during the Second World War.

The Church of the Good Shepherd in the village of Sion Mills, Co. Tyrone (1909 — W.F. Unsworth), is a wonderful surprise. Based on a church in Florence, it is in the Italianate Romanesque style and very striking in its setting. It is a large rectangular building with five huge, semicircular clerestory windows on each side of the nave. An arcaded apsidal staircase projects from the west wall, and at the east end is a campanile with a smaller square tower opposite. The interior is bright and spacious with the main emphasis on the chancel, which is reached by a flight of seven steps with a further three steps to the altar. The pulpit and lectern are of Connemara marble and are modelled on those in a church in Rome. Unsworth was also the architect of the Royal Shakespeare Theatre in Stratford-upon-Avon.

Christ Church, Derriaghy, Co. Antrim (1872 — William Gillespie), is a remarkable church with a west end unlike any other

110. (above) The Church of the Good Shepherd, Sion Mills, Co. Tyrone (1909).

111. (left) Christ Church, Derriaghy, Co. Antrim (1872).

in the country. Here the unusually tall, thin tower and the uncommonly slender spire stand at an angle of 45 degrees to the body of the church and are counterbalanced by a squat round turret which houses the stairs to the gallery. Between the two is a porch, above which is a crow-stepped gable, rarely seen in Ireland, incorporating an attractive circular window. The interior is equally surprising, with a steeply pitched pine roof shaped like an upturned boat with the chancel as its prow. The pews, also of pine, are well made, with a reputation for comfort. This is a singular building.

St Patrick's, Donaghpatrick, Co. Meath (1866 — J.F. Fuller), is situated at a crossroads, where it forms an attractive grouping with the parochial hall and sexton's house. It has a massive square medieval west tower (previously a four-storey private residence), to which the three-bay nave and chancel were added to form a pleasing and sturdy church. The interior includes stained glass by Sarah Purser and a sixteenth-century memorial in the chancel. Nearby is the site of the original Tailltean games.

St Anne's, Kilbarron (1841 — William Farrell), with its walls and tower of white harling, is conspicuously sited on a hill overlooking Ballyshannon, Co. Donegal. The tower is four-storey and contains a clock and peal of eight bells, while the main building is two-storey with ten mainly clear glass recessed windows on each floor. Internally it is high and spacious, with galleries on three sides which in earlier times accommodated the garrison of nearby Finner Army Camp. There are box pews, a font dated 1850 and a

112. St Patrick's Church, Donaghpatrick, Co. Meath (1866).

113. Christ Church, Corbally, Co. Tipperary (1847).

good collection of memorials, including one to Captain C. O'Neill, a Napoleonic War veteran.

Christ Church, Corbally, Co. Tipperary (1847), is an interesting building of unusual design. It was originally a mill, but as the flow of water was insufficient it never prospered. In 1829 it reopened as a church and in 1843, during a service with a congregation of nearly 400, the upper floor collapsed but without causing serious injury to those present. It was completely rebuilt by 1847, when the present tower and attractive belfry were added. Of two storeys, the parish hall is on the ground floor with the church above, adding practicality to its charm.

There are some churches whose very simplicity attracts attention, and St Molua's, Kyle, Co. Laois, is an excellent example. Externally this small whitewashed building looks like a farmhouse but has actually been in use as a church since about 1869 and doubled as the local school up to 1960. Leatbeg Church, West Fanad Peninsula, Co. Donegal, is another simple but appealing mid-nineteenth-century building, which was previously a schoolhouse.

Lurganboy Church, Co. Leitrim (1860), is a small, unassuming corrugated iron building and, possibly, the oldest structure of its kind in Ireland. In the nineteenth century this type of church was often prefabricated, and many were exported in flat-packs to the British colonies and elsewhere. A much more ambitious church of similar construction is St Peter's, Laragh, Co. Monaghan (1890), erected by a local mill-owner following his return from honeymoon in Switzerland where he is said to have got the idea for the design, described as light-hearted Gothic. This unique and romantic building, with its two-storey tower, slim spire, weather-vane and ornamental ridge crest, only lasted 80 years before it was deconsecrated and abandoned. By the year 2000 it was in a very poor state of repair and almost hidden by the encroaching woods which surround it, but it has now been listed by Monaghan County Council so that, hopefully, its future is assured.

By contrast, a handful of small but distinguished churches by the leading architects of their day are among the treasures of the Church of Ireland. St Patrick's, Adragh, near Carrickmacross, Co. Monaghan (1874 — William Slater), is one of these and was built at the sole expense of the Shirley family, who were local landowners. Described by Jeremy Williams as 'a modest masterpiece', it has a stone vaulted apse with a raised altar, underneath which is a hidden crypt. There is a rose window at the west end and fine stained glass in the attractive recessed windows in the nave and apse. This is a serene church, enhanced by the beauty of the marble font and the stone-carved pulpit with its shamrock decoration. Like other country churches, Adragh has a problem with bats and their droppings, the difficulty being that they are a protected species.

Abington Church, Abington, Co. Limerick (1870 — Rawson Carroll), is a beautiful, recently restored polychromatic church with a delightful tower and octagonal spire. The four-bay interior is also polychromatic, with the splendid three-light chancel window

114. Leatbeg Church, West Fanad Peninsula, Co. Donegal.

divided by slim marble colonettes and containing colourful stained glass. The recessed cusped windows in the nave are striking and also contain good stained glass, including one by A. E. Child. The ceiling is blue with gilded stars. A parishioner, Sir Charles Barrington, was one of the founders of the Irish Rugby Football Union while a student at Trinity College, Dublin.

Two other polychromatic churches worthy of mention are Ballyeglish Parish Church, the Loup, Co. Londonderry (1866–9 — Welland and Gillespie), and St Michael and All Angels, Whitegate, Co. Cork (1881 — William Atkins). Alistair Rowan describes the former as 'a stylish piece of roguery', while Jeremy Williams considers the latter to be 'challenging and discordant'. Certainly, neither is run-of-the-mill, and the same can be said for St Peter's, Carrigrohane, Co. Cork (1854 — Joseph Welland), with its long low nave and even lower side aisle with small rectangular windows added by William Burges in 1867. The off-centre tower and spire combine to form a church with an out-of-the-ordinary but pleasing interior.

115. (left) The abandoned Laragh Church, near Carrickmacross, Co. Monaghan.

116. (right) Abington Church, Abington, Co. Limerick (1870).

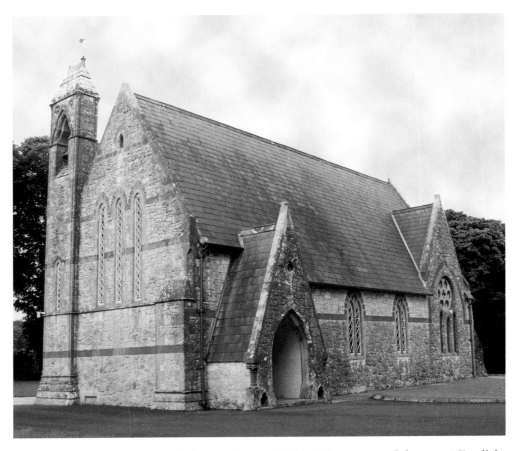

117. Ballyeglish Parish Church, the Loup, Co. Londonderry (1869).

George Edmund Street (1824–81) was one of the great English Gothic Revival architects and the man who rebuilt Christ Church Cathedral, Dublin, and Kildare Cathedral. He was also the architect of Fiddown Church, Piltown, Co. Kilkenny (1862), which has an unusual west end with a porch over which is a buttress flanked on both sides by three lancet windows with a rose window above. Internally the walls are of exposed stonework, and there is a beautiful chancel complemented by the good-quality pulpit, font, organ and memorials.

Street's only other Irish church is the Church of St John the Evangelist, Ardamine, Co. Wexford (1862), situated on an ancient motte overlooking the sea south of the seaside resort of Courtown Harbour. This is a delightful little church which, like Fiddown, has a buttress at the west end which supports a tiny spire complete with weather-vane. The stone-roofed southside porch leads into an interior which is only the length of a cricket pitch but splendid in every way. The walls are of exposed masonry and a perfect foil to the polychromatic brickwork in the chancel arch and window surrounds in the nave and apse. The window surrounds are particularly attractive, with arches supported by slender marble colonnettes. There is a timber roof in the nave and apse, each of different design, and a lovely pulpit and font, both of Caen stone.

118. The Church of St John the Evangelist, Ardamine, Co. Wexford.

12. NEW CHURCHES IN THE REPUBLIC OF IRELAND (1922–2000)

When Queen Victoria visited Dublin to a rousing reception in 1900, nobody could have foreseen that a mere 22 years later Ireland would be partitioned, having experienced in the interim a world war, a rebellion, a war of independence and a bitter civil war. For the more than 250,000 members of the Church of Ireland living in what was to become the Irish Free State and eventually the Republic of Ireland, these events were catastrophic. They found themselves, in 1922, a minority weakened by the murders, intimidation and destruction of property wreaked upon them during the previous six years, as well as the loss of thousands of their menfolk in the Great War and their abandonment by the king and country for whom these men had sacrificed their lives. Protestants found it difficult to adjust to the new regime in the years immediately following independence and many, chiefly for political and economic reasons, emigrated to Northern Ireland, Great Britain and the British dominions and colonies. By 1926 their numbers had fallen to 165,000. Those who remained gradually came to terms with the new administration, but the old vigour and confidence had disappeared and numbers continued to decline. This was partly due to the intolerance of a triumphalist and all-powerful Roman Catholic Church which, in a complete reversal of roles, brooked no opposition and was in every respect but name the new State Church. Its insistence that the children of a mixed marriage be brought up as Catholics caused great resentment because it was a major factor in further reducing the Protestant population, which in 1946 had fallen to 125,000 or less than half that of 1916.

This huge drop in numbers inevitably led to the closure of churches, a process which continued throughout the twentieth century. There had already been closures in the late nineteenth

119. Great War Memorial on the south wall of All Saints' Church, Grangegorman, Dublin.

120. Great War memorial to Lieutenant S.H. Lewis at St Multose's Church, Kinsale, Co. Cork.

century following emigration caused by the 'Land Wars' of 1879–82, but the situation was far more serious after 1922, when many congregations were reduced to a handful of families insufficient to support the maintenance of a church. No figures are available for the whole of the twentieth century, but 148 churches closed between 1956 and 1965 and about 200 between 1974 and 2000. Most of these losses were in rural areas but the cities also suffered. In 1900 there were six parish churches in Limerick but today only St Michael's, Pery Square (1844), remains open for worship. St Nicholas, Cove Street, Cork (1723), which could accommodate a congregation of over 1000, was deconsecrated in 1998. In Waterford only Christ Church Cathedral survives.

The deconsecration and closure of any church is a sad and traumatic experience for the inevitably small but loyal congregation. It is especially so for those elderly people who remember it in happier times. This was where they were baptised and married and where they expected to end their days. It was also where they met their neighbours every Sunday and held a central place in their lives and community. When the door closes for the last time it is not simply the church building which is lost, but the memorials and the gifts handed down over the generations in the form of stained glass, lecterns, altar cloth, communion plate and the like. This is the loss that so many members of the church have had to bear in the twentieth century and which is likely to continue because, despite the persistent culling, there are still too many churches.

However, all is not doom and gloom. Most of the cathedrals were refurbished in the latter part of the century and are now in excellent order, while some, like Christ Church, Dublin, report a marked increase in the number of regular worshippers. Many also attract large numbers of visitors. Numerous parish churches have been restored and redecorated, and some, like Knockbride near Shercock, Co. Cavan (1825), have installed floodlighting. Much of this work has only been possible as a result of the generous support of the Roman Catholic community and local government. The government also makes grants on a haphazard basis towards the often huge cost of repairing and restoring listed/heritage churches but, more often, the problem of finding the necessary money is left to the local congregation, which may be few in numbers with limited resources and already paying the crippling insurance premiums which these churches attract. The time is surely ripe for the state to accept full responsibility for the maintenance of such important and irreplaceable buildings.

About a dozen new churches were built after independence, including St Thomas's, Cathal Brugha Street, Dublin (1932 — Frederick G. Hicks), which replaced an eighteenth-century church destroyed in 1922 during the Civil War. It is a red-brick building in the Byzantine style, with a five-bay arcaded portico across the front, surmounted by a wheel window in the west gable, and with a bell-tower at the south-east corner. It is the venue for the 'I Believe' series of talks given by well-known Irish people and a reminder that many churches are used for concerts, recitals and the like. The acoustics of churches are often excellent, and their central position in cities and towns makes them easily accessible.

Frederick G. Hicks was also the architect of St Peter and St Paul, Kilmallock, Co. Limerick (1938), which replaced a previous church destroyed by fire in 1935. It is a red-brick, three-bay building with round-headed windows in the nave and a Modernist square west tower with large rectangular louvred upper windows. It was built with a blank east wall, but when the neighbouring Bruree church was closed Eamon de Valera (1882–1975), the then Irish taoiseach who lived nearby when a boy, was instrumental in having its stained glass east window removed and installed in the east wall of the Kilmallock church. He also subscribed generously to the cost.

St Mary's, Crumlin, Co. Dublin (1942 — Lionel Dixon), was

*121. St Thomas's
Church, Cathal
Brugha Street,
Dublin (1932).*

*122. Church of
SS Peter and
Paul, Kilmallock,
Co. Limerick
(1938).*

123. St Mary's Church, Crumlin, Co. Dublin (1942).

124. Christ Church, Spanish Point, Co. Clare (1927).

remarkably innovative at a time of extreme conservatism and is one of the earliest examples of new twentieth-century church architecture in Ireland. It was built externally and internally in an attractive burnt yellow brick (the last produced by the Dolphin's Barn brickworks) and is in the Modernist style with art deco metal windows and doors. The slightly tapering eastern bell-tower has clean lines but little decoration, while slim triangular buttresses relieve the planes of the north and south outer walls. The interior is bright and spacious with attractive contemporary furnishings. Close by is the eighteenth-century church where John Wesley preached. Following years of neglect and vandalism it has been restored as a community centre.

125. Church of the Transfiguration, Sneem, Co. Kerry (1967).

Christ Church, Spanish Point, Co. Clare (1927), replaces a church damaged by fire in 1922 and is an attractive building with a west tower and small broach spire overlooking a south porch. The roof, with a simple cross at each end, has red tiles, and these together with the white harled walls give it a cheerful Mediterranean appearance. The same is true of the Church of the Transfiguration, Sneem, Co. Kerry (1967), with its glass verandah-type porch, square tower surmounted by an octagonal tower, and tiny slated spire with salmon weather-vane. The entire exterior is white bordered with black, and a large palm tree in the drive adds to the feeling that this is not County Kerry but the south of France. It was built around the shell of an 1810 church and is said to have received its name because the rector on seeing the new building for the first time exclaimed 'It has been transfigured'. The bright interior is enhanced by the work of local craftsmen.

Christ Church, Shannon, Co. Clare (1961), is one of the few churches in the British Isles to be shared every Sunday by the Church of Ireland, Methodist and Presbyterian communities. It is a simple, rectangular, prefabricated building of red cedar wood

126. Christ Church, Shannon, Co. Clare (1961).

127. St Michael's Church, Killorglin, Co. Kerry (1997).

whose existence is entirely due to Shannon Airport. Previously the area was desolate moorland.

The last church built in the twentieth century was St Michael's, Killorglin, Co. Kerry (1997 — Peter O'Farrelly), which is part of the Kilcolman Social Centre incorporating three halls, meeting rooms, toilets, showers and a kitchen. It is a well-designed, single-storey, stone-faced building with a slated roof and pyramid-type structure over the main entrance. The atmosphere in the church is peaceful and intimate, and in line with modern trends the clergy are close to the congregation, with the seating converging on the altar.

13. NEW CHURCHES IN NORTHERN IRELAND (1922–2000)

Following the partition of the island in 1922 the Church of Ireland experience in Northern Ireland was quite different to that in the Irish Free State. The relatively small area covered by the six counties of Antrim, Armagh, Down, Fermanagh, Londonderry and Tyrone was home to 320,000 members in 1926 and this increased to 345,000 by 1937. They remained British citizens with a legislative assembly at Stormont described by its first prime minister, Sir James Craig, as 'a Protestant parliament for a Protestant people'. By contrast with their co-religionists in the south their way of life continued unchanged.

In the years between 1922 and 1939 about a dozen new churches were built in traditional styles. The most noteworthy are St Christopher's, Mersey Street, Belfast (1931 — Henry Seaver and R.H. Gibson), in a simple but perfectly proportioned Romanesque style, St Clement's, Templemore Avenue, Belfast (1928 — Blackwood and Jury), in a mixture of Tudor and Gothic, and St Polycarp's,

128. St Comgall's Church, Rathcoole, Belfast (1955).

129. (left) St Molua's Church, Upper Newtownards Road, Belfast (1962).

130. (below) The Church of the Pentecost, Cregagh, Belfast (1963).

Upper Lisburn Road, Belfast (1929 — Blackwood and Jury), which is largely Gothic. Two other churches worthy of mention, both by W.D.R. Taggart in the Gothic style, are St Finian's, Cregagh Park, Belfast (1930), and St Bartholomew's, Stranmillis Road, Belfast (1930).

Everything changed radically with the onset of the Second World War (1939–45), in which Northern Ireland played a notable role, being strategically very important to the Allies. Belfast suffered when it was heavily bombed by the German air force in the spring of 1941. One air raid in April of that year left 700 people dead and caused great destruction, including the loss of four Church of Ireland churches and damage to many more. Amongst those destroyed were Holy Trinity, Trinity Street (1843), and St Barnabas's, Duncairn Gardens (1893 — Henry Seaver). Only the tower and spire of St James's, Antrim Road (1871 — W.H. Lynn), remained standing.

In the immediate aftermath of the war much time and money was spent on repairing and restoring those churches such as St Patrick's, Newtownards Road (1893), and St Paul's, York Street (1851 — Sir Charles Lanyon), which had been extensively damaged. When this work was finally completed in 1954 there began a church-building boom which saw the erection of many new churches in Belfast and its suburbs. Some replaced those destroyed in the Blitz but most were needed because of a movement of population away from the inner city to new suburban estates.

These new churches were radically different to those which had gone before and heralded a completely new approach to ecclesiastical architecture. The leading Church of Ireland architect in Ulster was Denis O'D. Hanna (1901–71), who linked modernity with traditionalism and produced a variety of interesting and attractive buildings. St Comgall's, Carmeen Drive, Rathcoole, Belfast (1955), is two-storey with the parochial hall on the ground floor and the church above. It is a tall, compact building with round-headed windows at the west end and each side of the hall, and five clear glass dormer windows on each side of the roof. The latter is topped by a bellcote with a thin finial on top.

St Molua's, Upper Newtownards Road (1962), and the Church of the Pentecost, Mount Merrion Avenue, Cregagh (1963), also in Belfast, are two other noteworthy red-brick churches by the same architect. The main façade of both has a very vertical emphasis, and each is filled with plain glass except in the lower panel, suggesting that the inspiration may have been Coventry Cathedral

131. The Church of the Holy Trinity and St Silas, Ballysillan Road, Belfast (1958).

which was built at about the same time. St Molua's is capped by a tall slated finial flanked by two smaller ones, whereas the Cregagh church has a single thin spirelet which is a common feature of the new architecture. Hanna did much to encourage contemporary representational art and his churches include work by David Pettigrew, Desmond Kinney, Elizabeth Campbell and James McKendry.

He also built St Brendan's, Sydenham, Belfast (1963), which was of similar design to St Comgall's but completely destroyed in a fierce gale in January 1965. Another Ulster architect, Gordon K. McKnight, built a new church on the same site which was consecrated in 1967. It has a most attractive interior with internal buttresses pierced by side aisles and in the chancel a magnificent mural of the Last Supper by Desmond Kinney, salvaged from the previous church. There is a delightful Lady Chapel in the south-west corner with eleven glowing lancet stained glass windows by Neil Shawcross. The font and pulpit are of Newry granite. McKnight described his church as 'a building of modern character to fulfil present social and economical requirements unfettered by stylistic detail'. St Paul's (1964), his church at Lisburn, Co. Antrim, has a west front very similar to St Brendan's.

The same architect also designed St Columbas's, Loughgall Road, Portadown, Co. Armagh (1970), where the plan is symmetrical and laid out in the form of a Greek cross, the arms of which ascend towards the central crossing and soar from there in pyramid shape to a lantern light and copper cross 65ft above ground level. The six-panel copper entrance door depicts fabulous Celtic beasts and birds. This is another church which unites modern building techniques with traditional forms.

John MacGeagh (1901–85) built churches which were more traditional and neo-Gothic in style. Holy Trinity and St Silas, Ballysillan Road, Belfast (1956), is a six-bay red-brick building with very large round-headed clerestory windows, an attractive square eastern tower and an impressive western entrance approached by a flight of steps. The interior is bright and airy with unusually wide arches separating the nave and the aisles. Two of his churches replaced others destroyed during the German air raids. The first of these was St Barnabas's, Duncairn Gardens, Belfast (1956), and the second St Silas's, Cliftonville Road, Belfast (1958), each of which was built in rustic brick and a Modernist neo-Gothic Scandinavian style, with tall square towers free of ornamentation and clean pure lines. These innovative buildings became victims of the so-called 'Troubles' in the last three decades of the century when they were forced to close owing to a scattering of their congregations caused by fear and intimidation. St Silas's has since been demolished and St Barnabas's is a community centre with an emphasis on reconciliation. Many churches, of every denomination, have been subjected to sectarian and terrorist attack. A typical example is the Church of the Transfiguration, Newtownbreda Road, Belfast (1965), which, along with a nearby Presbyterian church, was destroyed by an IRA bomb in 1992. Happily, it was rebuilt the following year and is a good example of

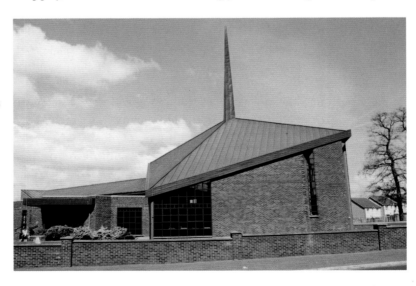

132. The Church of the Transfiguration, Newtownbreda Road, Belfast (1965).

133. St Andrew's Church, Glencairn Gardens, Belfast (1921). (Photo: Dr Ken Houston.)

a bright and cheerful modern church, with its metal-bound pews, altar, reading desk, chairs and roof all made of pine. Large clear glass windows the height of the walls allow the congregation to see the world outside and are an attractive feature.

Malicious damage, with no sectarian or political motive, is another problem faced by many churches. St Saviour's, Craigavon, Co. Armagh (1986 — G.P. and P.H. Bell), was badly vandalised in 1988 and 1992 but restored after each attack. Steel shutters front and rear are now necessary to help avoid a recurrence.

Only a handful of new churches were built in the western counties and three of these are in Derry, the best of which is St Peter's, Culmore Road (1967 — A.T. Marshall). Two were built in County Tyrone, namely Holy Trinity, Dromore (1957 — A.T. Marshall), a five-bay church with an asymmetrical square gabled tower, and St Andrew's, Clare (1996), a plain, white-walled building with a pointed roof.

Although new and novel, all of the above buildings, except St Saviour's, are immediately recognisable as churches which show flair and imagination from an architectural point of view. The same cannot be said for a good proportion of those built in the closing decades of the century, where there is often nothing to suggest the presence of a church or any kind of ecclesiastical building. Some could be mistaken for a school, office or tennis pavilion. Towers, spires, pinnacles or any type of decoration are completely absent with, often, a cross on the wall or nearby the only clue to its real identity. Perhaps, owing to the civil unrest, there has been a tendency to deliberately create buildings with a plain anonymous appearance to avoid attention. Often, however, these stark exteriors hide a bright and welcoming interior, as at St Andrew's, Glencairn Gardens, Belfast (1971), owned jointly by the Church of Ireland and the Methodist Church.

Finally, two buildings in Carrickfergus, Co. Antrim, exemplify different views of what a modern church should look like. St Colman's, Kilroot (1981), is a neat, well-built, single-storey, red-brick structure with a slate roof, yet completely unlike what would have been immediately recognisable as a church from the middle of the century or earlier. Internally it is simple and plain, with the altar in the centre surrounded on three sides by pews and with the choir behind. This layout represents a new spirit in worship with the clergy in close proximity to their congregation, leading to a more informal atmosphere than in the churches of the past. There is some stained glass from a previous church and a memorial to members of the Royal Ulster Constabulary killed during the Troubles. The rector of Kilroot in 1695–6 was the then-unknown Jonathan Swift.

Holy Trinity, Woodburn (1992), is the 27th church-cum-hall built in the Diocese of Connor since 1965 and one of the last erected in Northern Ireland in the twentieth century. It is a large, all-purpose building with a main hall, minor hall, office, vestry, meeting and computer rooms, kitchen and toilets. There is no church as such, the exterior giving little or no idea of what lies within. Church services are held in the main hall (which also acts as a badminton court and activity centre), while an adjoining stage separated from the hall by a folding partition doubles as the sanctuary. The latter contains an altar, a reading desk and the flags of the youth organisations. It is all very simple with an absence of decoration, and plans are in hand to extend the hall to further accommodate a rapidly increasing congregation.

These new buildings must make us wonder whether we still require churches to be beautiful and uplifting from an architectural point of view. In the twentieth century towers and spires went out of fashion and pinnacles were few and far between, which may reflect the fact that we no longer look to the heavens for salvation. Alternatively, the wheel may have turned full circle, and after the wonders of the Middle Ages, the splendours of the Georgian era and the inspiring Gothic of the nineteenth century we perhaps seek a return to the simple and unassuming architecture of Early Christian Ireland. It seems more likely, however, that when a new church is required, which may not be very often in the twenty-first century, the complex at Holy Trinity, Woodburn, will be the prototype. Whether or not this will be a matter for regret is for the reader to decide.

BIBLIOGRAPHY

Acheson, Alan 1997 *A history of the Church of Ireland.* Dublin.

Beckett, J.C. 1983 *William Burges and the building of St FinBarre's Cathedral.*

Benson, Rev. T.W. *Clanabogan Parish Church.*

Bowe, Nicola Gordon, Caron, David and Wynne, Michael 1998 *Gazetteer of Irish stained glass.* Dublin.

Bowen, Desmond 1978 *The Protestant Crusade in Ireland 1800–1870.* Dublin.

De Breffny, Brian and Mott, George 1976 *The churches and abbeys of Ireland.* London.

Brett, C.E.B. 1967 *Buildings of Belfast 1700–1914.* Belfast.

Brett, C.E.B. 1996 *Buildings of County Antrim.* Belfast.

Brett, C.E.B. 1999 *Buildings of County Armagh.* Belfast.

Byers, Robert 1968 *The Parish Church of St Mary, Belfast.* Belfast.

Carson, Derek 1999 *Christ Church, Castlebar — a brief history.*

Casey, Christine and Rowan, Alistair 1993 *The buildings of north Leinster.* London.

Condell, Rev. Joseph 1994 *St Cronan's, Roscrea — a brief history.*

Costello, Peter 1989 *Dublin churches.* Dublin.

Craig, Maurice 1989 John Semple and his churches. *Irish Arts Review.*

Craig, Maurice 1997 *The architecture of Ireland from the earliest times to 1800.* Dublin.

Dixon, Hugh 1975 *An introduction to Ulster architecture.* Belfast.

Dunlop, Robert 1982 *Plantation of renown — the La Touches of Harristown.*

Foster, R.F. 1989 *The Oxford illustrated history of Ireland.* Oxford.

Galloway, Peter 1992 *The cathedrals of Ireland.* Belfast.

Garrett, Arthur 1989 *Through countless ages.* Dublin.

Guinness, Desmond 1979 *Georgian Dublin.* London.

Harbison, Peter, Potterton, Homan and Sheehy, Jeanne 1978 *Irish art and architecture.* London.

Harvey, John 1949 *Dublin.* London.

Hewson, Adrian 1995 *Inspiring stones.*

Johnston, Sam 2001 *St Brendan's, Sydenham in the twentieth century.*

Keegan, Rev. Donald 1995 *St Brendan's, Birr — a brief history.*

Larmour, Paul 1987 *Belfast — an illustrated architectural guide.* Belfast.

Leland, Mary 1996 An Irishwoman's Diary. *Irish Times* (2 August 1996).

Lewis, Samuel 1846 *A topographical dictionary of Ireland.* London.

Longford, Elizabeth 1969 *Wellington — the years of the sword.* London.

MacCarthy, Canon Robert B. 1995 *Ancient and modern — a short history of the Church of Ireland.* Dublin.

Madden, Sydney R.W. and Parker, William 1987 *Ardamine and Killena parishes.*

Milne, Kenneth 1995 *The Church of Ireland — a history.* Dublin.

Muir, David 1996 *Christ Church, Delgany — a brief guide.*

Mullen, Rev. Charles 1997 *Christ Church, Gorey — a guide for visitors.*

Murphy, Tom 1989 *Adair Memorial Church 1889–1989.*

Myers, Kevin 1995 An Irishman's Diary. *Irish Times* (28 February 1995).

McCappin, Rev. William J. *St Patrick's Church, Jordanstown 1868–1993*.

O'Brien, Jacqueline and Guinness, Desmond 1994 *Dublin — a grand tour*. London.

Power, Denis and Sleeman, Mary *St Mary's Church, Doneraile*.

Reeves-Smyth, Terence 1990 *Crom Castle Demesne — a report in two volumes for the National Trust*.

Rothery, Sean 1993 *The buildings of Ireland*. Dublin.

Rowan, Alistair 1979 *The buildings of Ireland — north west Ulster*. London.

Ruddock, Norman and Kloss, Naomi 1997 *Unending worship — a history of St Iberius Church, Wexford*. Wexford.

Scott, Ernest V. 1993 *Churches of the Diocese of Connor*.

Scott, Kathleen A. 1948 *Christ Church, Bray — a guide for visitors*.

Scott, Rev. Lester 2001 *The Adelaide Memorial Church of Christ the Redeemer, Myshall*.

Shaffrey, Patrick and Shaffrey, Maura 1985 *Irish countryside buildings*. Dublin.

Sheehy, Jeanne 1980 *The rediscovery of Ireland's past — the Celtic Revival 1830–1930*. London.

Shepherd, Ernie 1983 *Behind the scenes— the story of Whitechurch, Co. Dublin*.

Stokes, A.E. 1983 *The Irish Heritage Series No. 12 — Christ Church Cathedral, Dublin*. Dublin.

Turner, Kathleen 1987 *Rathmichael — a parish history*.

Ulster Historical Society 1996 *Clergy of Down and Dromore*. Belfast.

Walker, Simon 2000 *Historic Ulster churches*. Belfast.

Williams, Jeremy 1994 *Architecture of Ireland 1837–1921*. Dublin.

The following publications are booklets and guides of varying sizes produced by the individual churches named:

All Saints', Raheny — A short guide (2001)
C.S. Lewis in St Mark's, Dundela — A short guide (1999)
Cathedral Church of St Anne, Belfast — A short guide (2001)
Christ Church, Leeson Park, Dublin — A brief history (2000)
Christ Church Cathedral, Lisburn — A brief illustrated guide (1993)
Christ Church Cathedral, Waterford — Visitor's guide
Church of the Resurrection, Blarney — Guide for visitors (1998)
Church of St Philip and St James, Holywood — A short illustrated guide (2000)
Coolcarrigan Church — Guide for visitors (1995)
Down Cathedral — Visitor's guide (1998)
Dromore Cathedral — Visitor's guide (2000)
Hillsborough Parish Church — An illustrated visitor's guide (2000)
Holy Trinity, Rathmines — A short guide (1991)
Holy Trinity, Westport — A guide for visitors (1998)
Parish of St Bartholomew, Dublin — An illustrated visitor's guide (2001)
Rosscarbery Cathedral — Visitor's guide (1999)
St Ann's, Dublin — Visitor's guide (1999)
St Audoen's, Dublin — Visitor's guide (2000)
St Brigid's Cathedral, Kildare — Visitor's guide (2000)
St Canice's Cathedral, Kilkenny — Visitor's guide (2000)
St Colman's Cathedral, Cloyne — Notes on the cathedral (2001)
St Columba's Cathedral, Londonderry — A short guide (2000)
St Columba's College Chapel, Dublin — Visitor's guide (2001)
St Flannan's Cathedral, Killaloe — Visitor's guide (1998)
St John's, Sandymount — A brief illustrated history (2001)
St Laserian's Cathedral, Old Leighlin — A short guide (1998)
St Mark's, Newtownards — A short guide (2000)
St Mary's Cathedral, Limerick — Booklet for visitors (1999)
St Maelruain's, Tallaght — A short guide (2001)
St Michan's, Dublin — Visitor's guide (2000)
St Multose, Kinsale — Visitor's guide (1992)
St Nicholas Collegiate Church, Galway — A short guide (1999)
St Patrick's Cathedral, Armagh — Visitor's guide (2001)
St Patrick's Cathedral, Dublin — Visitor's guide (1999)
St Peter's, Bandon — An illustrated guide (1999)
St Saviour's, Arklow — A guide for visitors (2000)
St Werburgh's, Dublin — Visitor's guide
The Friends of Monkstown Parish Church (1974)

The following were also useful sources of information:

The Automobile Association Book of Ireland (c. 1960)
Journal of the Irish Georgian Society
The Irish Builder
The Irish Architect
The Church of Ireland Gazette

GLOSSARY

ARCH	A curved structure spanning an opening or supporting a roof or floor.
AISLE	A passageway running parallel to the main span of a church.
ALTAR	Table used for the celebration of the Eucharist.
APSE	A large semicircular or polygonal recess at the eastern end of a church.
ARCADE	A series of arches supporting or set along a wall.
BALUSTER	Pillar or post supporting a rail or coping. A series of these form a **BALUSTRADE**.
BAPTISTRY	Area of a church where baptism is performed.
BATTLEMENT	A parapet with alternating indentations or embrasures and raised portions.
BAYS	The main vertical divisions of a building.
BELFRY	Bell-tower.
BELLCOTE	A frame on the gable of a roof in which a bell is hung.
BOSS	Ornamental knob or projection covering the intersection of ribs in a vault or ceiling.
BOX PEWS	Pews surrounded by tall timber-panelled partitions with a hinged door.
BROACH SPIRE	An octagonal spire on a square tower without a parapet and contained by four wedges of masonary at the base.
BUTTRESS	A mass of masonry or brickwork projecting from or built against a wall to give it additional strength.
CAMPANILE	See **BELFRY**.
CAPITAL	Head or top part of a column.
CASTELLATION	See **BATTLEMENT**.
CATHOLIC EMANCIPATION	Full civil and political rights for Roman Catholics.
CHANCEL	The east end of a church.
CLERESTORY	An upper storey, pierced by windows, in the main walls of a building.
COLONETTE	Small column.
COLUMN	An upright cylindrical pillar.
CORBEL	A projecting stone or timber for the support of a superincumbent weight.

CORINTHIAN	Fifth-century BC Classical order of architecture.
CRENELLATION	See **BATTLEMENT.**
CROW-STEPPED	The stepped tops of a church gable.
CROCKETS	Gothic decoration on the edge of a sloping feature.
CRUCIFORM	Church built in the shape of a cross.
CRYPT	Large vaulted chamber beneath a church.
DECORATED	English Gothic architecture, *c.* 1290–*c.* 1350.
DORIC	The earliest Classical order of architecture (*c.* sixth century BC).
EARLY ENGLISH	English Gothic architecture, 1200–50.
FAÇADE	The front or face of a building.
FENESTRATION	The arrangement of windows on a building.
FINIAL	An ornament at the top of a gable, canopy, pinnacle, etc.
FONT	Mounted vessel containing water used in the sacrament of baptism.
GABLET	Small gable-shaped top to a buttress.
GARGOYLE	A decorated water-spout projecting from a roof.
GIBBS SURROUND	Surround of door or window designed by James Gibbs (1682–1754).
GOTHIC	The architecture of the pointed arch developed from the twelfth century.
GREAT WAR	The 1914–18 World War.
HAMMERBEAMS	Horizontal brackets of a roof projecting at wall-plate level.
HARLED	Roughcast.
HIBERNO-ROMANESQUE	Style of ecclesiastical buildings in Ireland from the tenth to the twelfth century.
HIGH CROSS	A free-standing detached sculpted stone cross.
IONIC	Sixth-century BC Classical order of architecture.
LANCET	A tall, narrow window with a pointed head.
LECTERN	Reading stand to hold a copy of the Bible.
LIGHT	Compartment of a window.
LINTEL	A horizontal beam or stone over an opening.
LOUVRE	An opening fitted with sloping boards (or louvres) in the belfry of a church tower.

LUCARNE	Dormer window on a roof or spire.
MISERICORD	Mercy-seat or miniature ledge on the underside of hinged medieval choir-stall seats.
MODERNISM	Twentieth-century architectural movement that sought to sunder all stylistic and historic links with the past.
MULLION	A vertical post or upright dividing an opening with lights.
NAVE	The western section of a church, often flanked by aisles.
OCULUS	A circular opening in a wall.
OGHAM	Ancient Celtic alphabet of twenty letters dating from the fifth–seventh centuries.
PEDIMENT	A low-pitched gable used in Classical and Renaissance architecture above a portico or other feature.
PERPENDICULAR	The last of the Gothic architectural styles, *c.* 1400–1550.
PILASTER	A shallow rectangular column attached to a wall.
PINNACLE	Ornamental pyramid or cone.
PLANTER'S GOTHIC	A type of Gothic church built by Protestant settlers in Ulster in the seventeenth century.
POLYCHROMATIC	The use of many colours, usually for external architectural decoration, often describing brickwork in Victorian buildings.
PORTICO	A covered entrance supported by columns.
PULPIT	An elevated stand of stone or wood for a preacher.
REREDOS	A wall or screen of stone or wood, rising behind an altar or communion table.
ROMANESQUE	Style of architecture prevalent in Europe *c.* 900–*c.* 1200.
ROUND TOWER	Tall (average height 30m) tenth- to twelfth-century free-standing circular towers with a conical roof unique to Ireland. Used, *inter alia*, as a watch-tower.
SANCTUARY	Area around the altar or communion table of a church.
SEDILIA	Series of stone seats set in the south wall of the chancel.
SOUNDING-BOARD	A canopy over a pulpit.
STUCCO	Plaster used for coating wall surfaces or moulding into architectural decorations.
TESTER	See **SOUNDING-BOARD**.

TRACERY	Ornamental stone openwork especially in the upper part of a Gothic window.
TRACTARIANISM	A movement within the Church of England stressing its links with Catholic Christianity.
TRANSEPT	The arms of a cross-shaped church.
TUSCAN	The least ornamented order of Classical architecture.
TYMPANUM	The triangular or semicircular field in the face of a pediment or in the head of an arch.
VAULT	An arched ceiling or roof of stone or brick, sometimes imitated in wood and plaster. Also used to refer to a place of burial beneath a church.
VENETIAN WINDOW	A three-light window with a tall round-headed middle light and shorter lights on either side.
VESTRY	A room in a church for sacred vessels and vestments.

Gazetteer of Cathedrals and Churches

County Antrim
All Saints', Antrim 17
Ballinderry Parish Church, Ballinderry *16*, 60
Ballintoy Parish Church, Ballintoy 62
Christ Church Cathedral, Lisburn 23, 126
Christ Church, Derriaghy 108, 109
Duneane Church, Duneane 48
Holy Trinity, Ballycastle *40*, 41
Holy Trinity, Carrickfergus 130–1
Middle Church, Ballinderry 15, *16*
St Bride's, Doagh 91
St Colman's, Carrickfergus 130
St John's, Islandmagee 14, *15*
St Nicholas's, Carrickfergus 13, 15
St Patrick's, Armoy *60*, 61
St Patrick's, Jordanstown 98, *99*
St Paul's, Lisburn 127
St Thomas's, Rathlin Island 71

County Armagh
Archbishop Robinson's Chapel, Armagh *45*, 47
Church of Christ the Redeemer, Lurgan 91
Creggan Parish Church, near Crossmaglen 51
Holy Trinity, Drumsallan 59
St Columbas's, Portadown 127
St John's, Lisnadill 56–7
St Luke's, Ballymoyer 90
St Luke's, Mullaghglass 63
St Mark's, Armagh 63, *64*
St Patrick's Cathedral, Armagh 8
St Saviour's, Craigavon 129

Belfast
Cathedral Church of St Anne 29, *30*, *31*
Christ Church, College Square North (deconsecrated) 40
Church of the Pentecost, Mount Merrion Avenue 126
Church of St John the Evangelist, Malone Road 90
Church of the Transfiguration, Newtownbreda Road 128
Holy Trinity, Trinity Street (destroyed in 1941) 126
Holy Trinity and St Silas's, Ballysillan Road 126, *127*, 128
Knockbreda Parish Church, Newtownbreda *39*, 41

INDEX OF ARCHITECTS

General index